The Inequalities

The Inequalities

Beyond Caring
LOVE
Faith, Hope and Charity

ALEXANDER ZELDIN

Edited by
FAYE MERRALLS

methuen | drama
LONDON • NEW YORK • OXFORD • NEW DELHI • SYDNEY

METHUEN DRAMA
Bloomsbury Publishing Plc
50 Bedford Square, London, WC1B 3DP, UK
1385 Broadway, New York, NY 10018, USA
29 Earlsfort Terrace, Dublin 2, Ireland

BLOOMSBURY, METHUEN DRAMA and the Methuen Drama logo are trademarks of
Bloomsbury Publishing Plc

First published in Great Britain 2022

A catalogue record for this book is available from the British Library.

A catalog record for this book is available from the Library of Congress.

ISBN: PB: 978-1-3502-7177-7
ePDF: 978-1-3502-7178-4
eBook: 978-1-3502-7179-1

Typeset by RefineCatch Limited, Bungay, Suffolk

To find out more about our authors and books visit www.bloomsbury.com
and sign up for our newsletters.

Contents

Foreword

The Inequalities

Rufus Norris

I met Alex for the first time on the balcony outside the staff canteen. He'd made *Beyond Caring* at the Yard Theatre in 2014 and was at the NT to remount it in the Shed, our temporary theatre, a year later. I liked him instantly – his heart, politics and mind passionately grappling with whatever section of the play he was still cooking. A week or so later *Beyond Caring* opened, a pure and fearless work, unflinching in its gaze at the zero-hours reality that is all around us. The audience were grimly and utterly spellbound. One of them fainted. We grabbed a brief moment after the show (literally behind the Shed) and stayed there for an hour or more, arguing and agreeing in equal measure. That conversation has continued unabated since, while he has made the NT his home and evolved this very particular dramatic enquiry.

LOVE opened at the end of 2016, and *Faith, Hope and Charity* followed three years later. Both were created in his very particular style: distilled slowly from a great deal of research and structured workshops with a small, excellent group of actors, a balance of professionals and people drawn from the communities he was exploring.

LOVE observes a small group of people thrown together in temporary accommodation. Unintended abrasions and unlikely alliances interweave and unfold in micro-observation, building imperceptibly as Christmas approaches.

Faith, Hope and Charity goes a step further and witnesses the last months in the life of a community hall, illuminating the diverse assembly who make use of it and for whom it becomes a sanctuary of this time.

All three are fiercely political, but no tables are thumped, no misery indulged, no saccharine sprinkled. His complete absorption in the places and people from which his stories are drawn prevents them from ever tipping into cliché, never allowing the audience the comfort of distance as the harsh imbalance of our twenty-first-century society plays out through a multitude of small acts: of need, rejection, friendship, humiliation and kindness in a microcosm of our destructive yet hopeful humanity.

At one point during a performance of *LOVE*, an audience member leapt impulsively from his seat to prevent a tragedy in miniature unfolding in front of him. The fourth wall that separates the actor from the audience had long since dissolved. For all its ultra-realism, Alex's unique voice is profoundly theatrical, both a celebration of and testament to that live, human, imaginative exchange.

Introduction to *Beyond Caring*: 'How Does Theatre Represent Economic Systems?'

Louise Owen

This Introduction was previously published in *Thinking Through Theatre and Performance* (Methuen, 2019)

This chapter explores theatre's inextricable engagement with economic systems and their roles and structures. Economy is an expansive historical term, meaning 'the way in which something is managed; the management of resources; household management'. One of the term's roots, the ancient Greek *oikonomia*, also more broadly signifies 'administration, principles of government, arrangement of a literary work, stewardship' (*Oxford English Dictionary* 2018). Economic systems thus concern more than matters of 'wealth generation' alone, and are based on ideas concerning how societies should be organized and the functions people should assume within them; as Wendy Brown puts it, using theatrical metaphor, 'the casting of economic life' (Brown 2015: 83). And the histories studied in our classrooms demonstrate multiple concrete interactions between theatre and economy: for example, the social mandate in ancient Athens to attend theatre festivals and the display of imperial tribute that was made beforehand, the role of trade guilds in supporting mystery cycles in medieval England, or the colonial imposition and control of theatre institutions in twentieth-century Kenya (Goldhill 1997: 56; King 2006: 10–12; Wa Thiong'o 1986: 38–41). As well as what is performed on stage, theatre is implicated in the material functioning of culture and society through its institutions, the representational practices and political struggles those institutions involve, and the identities and ideologies they stage. In other words, as institution, theatre plays its part in processes of *social reproduction* both on and off stage – an emphatically economic question. As Silvia Federici argues (writing specifically on domestic labour), 'the reproduction of human beings is the foundation of every economic and political system' (2012: 2). Ric Knowles thus theorizes what he calls the *material theatre* in terms of a contextual 'triangle' of 'complex and coded systems – of production, theatrical communication and reception, all working in concert or in tension with one another' (Knowles 2004: 3). And Miranda Joseph's recommendation that we pay attention to 'sign production as well as material production . . . the performativity of production, of the circulation of social formations as well as goods' (2002: 67) resonates with Knowles's critical practice.

In this sense, a particular theatre piece need not explicitly address economic issues, nor adhere to a particular aesthetic or genre, to be engaged in economic themes – just as a piece that claims to be doing so may be up to something quite different. Here, I discuss a piece that does explicitly dramatize a contemporary industrial context: Alexander Zeldin's *Beyond Caring* (2014–16), a hyper-naturalistic work set in a meat factory. For Zeldin, if the show is 'about' anything, it is about 'very tender moments of connection between isolated people' (personal interview 2016). With this statement in view, I analyse how the piece represents, and thinks through, industrial capitalism and its social relationships. Political theorist and historian Ellen Meiksins Wood offers this essential definition of capitalism: 'a system in which goods and services, down to the most basic necessities of life, are produced for profitable exchange, where even human labour-power is a commodity for sale in the market, and where all economic actors are dependent on the market' (Meiksins Wood [1999] 2002: 2). Put in Marxian terms, capitalism is a particular *mode of production*: a way of organizing society and its resources 'structured according to its class relations' (Fine & Saad-Filho 2004: 6). In what follows, I examine the techniques that *Beyond Caring* uses in representing the experience of insecure factory work in Britain under the conditions of austerity. By way of comparison, I briefly discuss *The Pajama Game* (1954), an example of mid-twentieth-century musical theatre, also set in a factory, whose plot concerns industrial action. Throughout, the chapter is geared towards a particular question: what do *Beyond Caring*'s representational strategies reveal about the continuities of the capitalist system across the decades, and how theatre makers have chosen to respond to it?

Beyond Caring in performance

Alexander Zeldin's *Beyond Caring* was first presented at the Yard Theatre, Hackney in 2014. It then ran at the National Theatre Temporary Space in 2015, and in 2016, it undertook a UK national tour to Birmingham REP, Theatre Delicatessen in Sheffield and HOME in Manchester, also playing a European date at Les Théâtres de la Ville de Luxembourg. In 2017, Zeldin reworked the piece for a North American context with Lookingglass Theatre in Chicago. I first saw the production at the National Theatre Temporary Space on Saturday 2 May 2015. It was five days before the 2015 General Election. Between 2014 and 2015, the number of people employed on a zero hours contract – 'a colloquial term for a contract of service under which the worker is not guaranteed work and is paid only for work carried out' (Pyper and Brown 2016: 4) – had reportedly risen by 100,000 to around 697,000 (Inman 2015). In 2017, that figure rose still further, to 910,000 (Monaghan 2017). On the basis of the expansion of low-paid, insecure jobs, and the linked increase of 'underemployment' (Bell and Blanchflower 2013), Labour had made a manifesto commitment to 'ban exploitative zero hours contracts' (Labour Party 2015: 37). In the lobby of the National Theatre Temporary Space, a chalkboard bore a statement on zero hours contracts from the most recent edition of BBC *Question Time* – a small business owner's hostile response to Labour's proposed ban – and an annotation, presumably authored by someone at the National Theatre, attacking Labour hypocrisy concerning MPs' use of this type of contract. The chalkboard's presentation of topical information framed the production as a contribution to a live political debate whose outcome would affect the types of lives represented in *Beyond Caring* – those of people struggling to make ends meet by subsisting on insecure low-paid work – though the statements seemed to align the National Theatre both with the small business owner, whose words received no commentary, and against Ed Miliband's Labour and its moves to redress the exploitations of underemployment.

   Thinking on the chalkboard and its contradictory effects, I took my seat in the Temporary Space. Arranged in a thrust configuration, with the audience on three sides both on the ground floor and in the gallery, the stage offered up the bleak, acutely realistic interior of a factory break room in 'a small loading bay area' (Zeldin 2015: 2). Its dark grey floor was stained with what resembled dried coffee, as if someone had

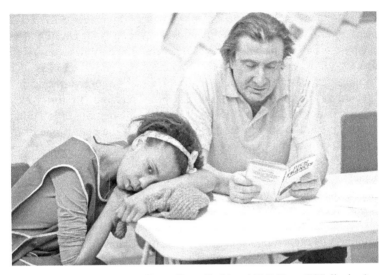

Figure 1 *Beyond Caring*. Grace (Janet Etuk) and Phil (Sean O'Callaghan).
Photo: Mark Douet.

kicked over a disposable cup a while ago and not bothered to wipe up the spillage. Some plastic office chairs were clustered around a pale grey trestle table, a few items of rubbish scattered across its surface and the surrounding floor. The back wall, a grimy shade of beige, bore large dark stains. A double door dead centre, flanked by a tall plastic bin, indicated a further room beyond, in which a health and safety poster and a fire bucket were visible. In the break room itself, two tall metal trolleys were standing against the wall behind the trestle table, filled with bin bags and folded up cardboard boxes. An adjacent noticeboard displayed a smattering of notices, all on white paper. Immediately behind the audience, on the upstage left side, was a small atrium containing coat hooks and an automatic coffee machine with a garish orange neon display – the only source of colour in the whole environment. And in the parallel spot, upstage right, was a wooden pallet, shrink-wrapped in clear plastic, upon which rested a batch of large white plastic containers of cleaning fluid. Casting my eyes to the gallery, I noticed a metal ladder and vacuum cleaner resting against a similarly grimy wall. The overall effect was drab and miserable, made all the more harsh by the cold strip lighting that illuminated the stage space, and the white floods that kept the audience in light throughout the performance. Seated in close proximity to the action, it was as if we, the audience, were in the midst of the factory break room. Another striking feature was the way in which this scenography segued seamlessly into other parts of the Temporary Theatre Space. Before the performance began, beyond the room containing the fire bucket, the cheery red of the theatre's foyer could be seen through another door, pointing to a world beyond.

In this dismal situation, we meet the characters. Three women who are employed by agencies (Grace, Becky and Susan) join a permanent, part-time member of staff (Phil, formerly a nurse) and a tyrannical middle manager (Ian) to work in the factory, which makes processed meat products. The agency workers have been recruited, as Ian explains, to 'a fourteen consecutive day position' (Zeldin 2015: 7) cleaning the factory

– work that is to take place at night. The play consists dramaturgically of a series of scenic episodes, unfolding in a linear temporality, structured by the cleaning assignment. Full blackouts and a machinic bass-heavy roar separate the episodes, constructing them as fragmentary glimpses of a world. In common with many thousands of disabled people in the context of the Coalition government, Grace has been affected by changes to rules regarding disability benefit: she has been declared 'fit for work' despite suffering from rheumatoid arthritis. Becky is a young mother. Susan is a middle-aged woman whose attempt to stay in the factory to sleep at the end of one of the shifts suggests homelessness. The play does not belabour this information: these details emerge piecemeal as the drama plays out, along with others that lend texture and depth to the characters' lives – for example, that Grace needs to take two buses to and from work, and that she attends church.

Each scene takes its time. They trace out the agency workers' peremptory introduction to the job by Ian, their fifteen-minute breaks (some interrupted by work), and the beginnings and ends of their punishing shifts. The play's action is sombre, but studded with moments of dark humour. Extended silences punctuate the characters' jarring attempts at social interaction during their breaks, making the moments in which the characters do make friendly connections with one another all the more poignant and hopeful. When those relationships fail or falter – as with a moment of unpleasant irritation that sabotages a growing friendship between Grace and Phil, provoked by a manipulative divide-and-rule tactic by Ian – the effect is heart-breaking. We, the audience, witness those relationships developing in what feels like real time, which compounds the feelings of sympathy they induce. Losses pervade the characters' lives relative to this situation: Becky and Phil, of contact with their children; Grace, of disability support and contact with her church community. As the action plays out, it is not clear which day of the fourteen-day clean it is – and it is as if this really doesn't matter, that time will be felt as excruciating whatever day it is. The play's conclusion, in which 'isolated people get too close to one another, too fast' (Zeldin 2015), sees the construction of a warped familial scene. Bullied into work by Ian when she is unwell, Grace experiences a distressing seizure, and is comforted and soothed to sleep by Phil. Seemingly compelled by this evidence of his kindness, Becky reaches to Phil in desperation, and they copulate on the factory floor – an event that is witnessed by no one, and which therefore catalyses nothing within the wider world of the play. The final image is of all the workers, middle manager Ian included, furiously scrubbing a filthy piece of equipment, before a blackout plunges the scene into darkness.

Representing the factory

The small kindnesses and cruelties of *Beyond Caring*'s characters, playing out in the hostile environment of the factory, pack a powerful emotional punch. But in what ways can we interpret the play as concerned with everyday human relationships, *and* the wider economic system? Why is it not only about the social aspects of friendship, or the abuse of power? To approach this question, it's necessary to situate the play's setting in a wider historical and material context. *Beyond Caring*'s opening stage directions describe its setting as 'a meat factory (but it could be any other kind of industry) somewhere on the edges of a city in the western world' (Zeldin 2015: 2). The point, then, is not that we are witnessing work connected with meat processing specifically, although that metaphor is highly suggestive. We are watching action in a contemporary Western factory – a systematized, machinic institution whose massive expansion during the eighteenth and nineteenth centuries was critical in the development of industrialization. The factory, and the factory system, is a crucial element of the capitalist *means of production* – that is, the 'tools and raw materials' (Fine and Saad-Filho 2004: 24) used to make products and thus to generate profit. These raw materials include waged labour – a commodity that is vulnerable to harsh exploitation to maximize returns. Discussing the early-nineteenth-century textile industry in the north of England, historian Eric Hobsbawm gives this account of the factory: 'a logical flow of processes, each with a specialized machine tended by a specialized "hand", all linked together by the inhuman and constant pace of the engine and the discipline of mechanization, gas-lit, iron-ribbed and smoking . . . a revolutionary form of work' (1969: 68). He notes that many 'were pressed into the new system against their will and got nothing from it but pauperization'; further, given the loss of autonomy factory work imposed, men were more likely to decline such work where they could, entailing that it was fulfilled by 'the more tractable women and children' (1969: 66, 68).

In writing 'The Working Day', the tenth chapter of *Capital Volume I* (1867), Marx drew on the extensive reports of factory inspectors, produced in enforcing the Factory Acts imposed by the British government from 1833 onwards, which detailed unspeakable working conditions endured by adults and children in a number of industries – both in terms of physical danger and the exploitation of workers' time. According to Marx's analysis, the profit, or surplus value, generated from the sale of commodities is a function of what he calls the *socially necessary labour time* to make them: as Ben Fine and Alfredo Saad-Filho explain, 'the amount of labour time required to bake a loaf of bread when contrasted with that required to sew a shirt (and more importantly, how these labour times are determined and modified through technological and other changes)' (2004: 19). Any labour time afforded by the worker surplus to these amounts within the working day can be taken as profit – entailing sly and subtle claims on workers' spare time, which, Marx noted, were characterized by the factory inspectors as ' "petty pilferings of minutes" ' ([1867] 1990: 352) from their break and meal-times. In David Harvey's account, the introduction of state regulation to privately owned industry as the nineteenth century unfolded was a combined political outcome of pressure from a developing working-class movement, 'bourgeois reformism' responding to egregious factory practices, and the pragmatic requirement from the point of view of the state that the labour force not be run irretrievably into the ground (2010: 141–3). Regulation met considerable resistance from capital until factory owners recognized later in the nineteenth century that 'a healthy and efficient labour force, on a shorter working day, could be more productive than an unhealthy, inefficient, falling-apart, constantly turning over and dying off labour force' (Harvey 2010: 155).

Moving forward sixty years and crossing continents, let's turn briefly to *The Pajama Game*, a musical comedy about an industrial dispute between management and workforce in a mid-western garment factory, first staged on Broadway in 1954. It provides an interesting comparator to *Beyond Caring* not only because of its factory setting – it was revived by Chichester Festival Theatre in 2013 in a production directed by Richard Eyre and transferred to London's Shaftesbury Theatre in the West End in 2014, the same year that *Beyond Caring* was first produced. *The Pajama Game* resonates strongly with the economic conditions of the mid-twentieth century – that is, the moment following the devastation of the Second World War during which capital entered into more co-operative arrangements with organized labour in the interests of rebuilding and expansion (Harvey 1990: 125–40). Embodying this co-operation is the turbulent centrepiece love affair that takes place between trade unionist Babe and factory superintendent Sid, representatives of workforce and management. Immediately following the overture, as a musical vamp plays on underneath, factory timekeeper Hines tips his hat and announces to the audience:

> This is a very serious drama. It's kind of a problem play. It's about Capital and Labour. I wouldn't bother to make such a point of all this except later on if you happen to see a lot of naked women being chased through the woods, I don't want you to get the wrong impression. This play is full of SYMBOLISM.
>
> (Adler, Ross, Abbott and Bissell 1954: 5)

My friend Robin delivered these lines with aplomb in his performance of the role in our school production in 1996. In 2017, reading them again in my copy of the libretto, the cheeky wit of the text struck me in a manner lost on me at the time. Hines's exaggerated invocation of 'SYMBOLISM' along with the genre of the 'problem play' squarely positions *The Pajama Game* in a tongue-in-cheek dialogue with Henrik Ibsen – a nineteenth-century playwright whose naturalistic work explored social and cultural conflicts, especially those underpinned by class and wealth.

Ibsen was one of a number of nineteenth-century European dramatists and theatre makers contributing to the radical new transnational movement of theatrical naturalism – famous among them, Emile Zola, Anton Chekhov and August Strindberg. Naturalistic drama was paradoxically anti-theatrical: it refused received nineteenth-century stage convention and sought instead to present the authentic dynamics of everyday social interactions on stage through close observation and imitation. Of his play *Ghosts* (1881), Ibsen argued that its impact 'depends a great deal on making the spectator feel as if he were actually sitting, listening, and looking at events happening in real life' (Ibsen in Williams 1994: 172) – an assessment that also articulates a relationship between actors and audience wherein, as Nicholas Ridout puts it, 'one group of people spend leisure time sitting in the dark to watch others spend their working time under lights pretending to be other people' (2006: 6). This humorous description is historically specific: it conjures social constructions of work and leisure that emerged decisively in the nineteenth century, the economic positions of actors and audience, and also the genre of realism – actors are 'pretending to be other people' who might believably resemble those in the audience or elsewhere in society. Ridout points out that this is 'what we routinely understand theatre to be, in Western industrial or post-industrial modernity' (2006: 6) – that is, lights down, curtain up and audience silent in anticipation of entertainment and diversion. However, nineteenth-century naturalism was anxious to expose to public view 'the minutiae of everyday life' (Harvie and Allain 2006: 178), which also involved confronting its unpalatable aspects: corruption, violence, debt, disease. *The Pajama Game*'s satirical nod to Ibsen tells us something about the historical position of naturalism in representing social antagonism and seems to set off its own status as a comedy in doing so.

The saucy reference to the woods, meanwhile, reminds us definitively that *The Pajama Game* is an example of the popular commercial genre of musical comedy. The producers of the original show clearly recognized the marketing power of sexual imagery and the double entendre of 'pajama game': the 1954 Broadway poster features a cartoon woman wearing only a man's pyjama jacket, head demurely downcast but ample cleavage exposed, being ogled by the disembodied heads of five men while a sixth averts his gaze. This sexist image bears no actual relation to the plot – though in the show's fashion parade finale, the warring protagonist lovers demonstrate their reconciliation by sporting one pyjama set between them, confirming in song that 'Married life is lots of fun / Two can sleep as cheap as one' (Adler, Ross, Abbott and Bissell 1954: 51). Contradictorily, Babe's characterization as trade unionist gently subverts normative ideas of 1950s femininity, despite the show's fundamental commitment to the nuclear family as a structure – and as Jennifer L. Borda argues, at the end 'she comes to accept patriarchal society's definition of herself' (2010: 242). Following disruptions to the factory's Fordist production line and much interpersonal conflict, the world of the drama is finally rebalanced: corporate lies about profit and loss have been exposed, and the workers' demand for a modest pay rise satisfied. The concluding reprise of the song 'Seven and a Half Cents' triumphantly proclaims that the pay rise will have each member of the workforce 'Livin' like a King!' (Adler, Ross, Abbott and Bissell 1954: 51).

First-hand experience

The resolution represented in this Broadway musical is a far cry from the twenty-first-century circumstances represented in *Beyond Caring* – a much smaller scale production developed initially for a fringe space, and which drew extensively on first-hand accounts of insecure work in its research and development process. Zeldin encountered French journalist Florence Aubernas's *The Night Cleaner* (2010) in formulating another, unrealized show about youth unemployment; British writer Ivor Southwood's *Non-Stop Inertia* (2011) was recommended to him by a journalist friend (personal interview 2016). Inspired by these texts, *Beyond Caring* focuses on the cleaning of the factory – in other words, *reproductive labour*, an aspect critical to its action. As Andrew Herod and Luis L. M. Aguiar write, cleaning is 'essential to ensuring that the spaces of production, consumption, and social reproduction which define the social architecture of the contemporary global economy remain sanitary and functional' (2016: 427). Despite its crucial role, this kind of work is relegated to the time of day that least interrupts production and therefore the pursuit of profit, with the use of the shift-system that Marx argued enables 'appropriation of labour throughout the whole of the 24 hours in the day' ([1867] 2010: 367).

Aubernas and Southwood provide ample evidence of exploitative 'sweatshop' (Herod and Aguiar 2016: 426) practices and the 'existential vulnerability' (Southwood 2011: 16) of insecure work. Their texts also demonstrate the ways in which austerity – the policy of 'deliberate deflation of wages and prices through cuts to public spending' (Blyth 2013: 41) imposed in Britain and across Europe in response to the financial crisis – has affected the form and availability of unskilled work. They lend support to David

Harvey's conclusion that 'sad to report, Marx's analysis is all too relevant to our contemporary condition' (2010: 160). Aubernas undertook covert research into cleaning work in Basse-Normandie in northern France during the 2009 'recession'. She dyed her hair blonde, and masqueraded as a middle-aged divorcee with only a secondary qualification who was in desperate need of work. Sticking carefully to her story – 'I met a man who kept me, then ditched me' (Aubernas [2010] 2011: 21) – her mission was to be offered a permanent contract of employment. Chasing scant shifts of as little as ninety minutes, and competing for them with many other unemployed people, this is a very difficult goal. In the work she does get, overtime goes unpaid, hours of travel to and from work are completely unsubsidized, and employers place unsustainable demands on the speed of work itself in their bids to compete with other cleaning businesses. The emotional toll for workers is a constant sense of unease: 'a nagging anxiety on top of the basic tiredness that you can't get over' (Aubernas [2010] 2011: 207).

Meanwhile, Southwood suggests that this condition of anxiety about survival induces a paradoxical 'frenetic inactivity: we are caught in a cycle of non-stop inertia', concluding that the contemporary culture of work thrives on workers' 'immersive identification' (Southwood 2011: 11, 84) with it. Following Brecht's use of *Verfremdung*, or 'distantiation', he calls for the assumption of a critical stance in relation to this 'ideological theatre of employment' (Southwood 2011: 82). Brecht's translator, John Willett, explains that *verfremdung* constitutes 'not simply the breaking of illusion (though that is one means to the end); and it does not mean "alienating" the spectator in the sense of making him hostile to the play. It is a matter of detachment, of reorientation' (Willett [1959] 1977: 177). In his important essay, 'The Modern Theatre is the Epic Theatre' (1930), Brecht argued for making the spectator an 'observer' of human action represented on the stage, outlining various dramaturgical techniques to that end. He contrasted this effect with 'dramatic theatre', which, he proposed, positioned the spectator 'in the thick of it' (2001: 37). This metaphor resonates strongly with both contemporary forms of immersive theatre, which physically plunge spectators into theatrically constructed worlds, and the culture of work that Southwood critiques. Southwood argues that 'to short-circuit this cycle of inertia and truly move forward, we have to resist the pressure to go with the flow' (2011: 88) – in other words, to detach from its frenetic dynamics and to understand them not as natural or given, but as actively constructed and therefore changeable.

Beyond Caring's uses of silence and social awkwardness stage a critique of this 'ideological theatre of employment'. Its process of creation sought, as Zeldin puts it, to 'describe as intensely as possible how these fragilised people live their lives' (Zeldin quoted in Chakrabortty 2015: 33). With Athena Athanasiou, it is important to point out the depth of systemic inequality: 'the lives of those working in the cleaning sector, which is socially disdained as *par excellence* female and migrant labour, are precarious, dispensable, and disposable' (Athanasiou 2011). All *Beyond Caring*'s temporary agency workers are female, and the permanent staff members are male. But Zeldin was very clear that the aim with *Beyond Caring* was not to transmit a direct political agenda or message. Instead, his intention was to make a piece of theatre that 'works on the frame of a moment: inside that moment is contained all of a bigger moment, a bigger structure' (personal interview 2016). In developing material about exploitation, he observes that 'it's more interesting for us to look at what the *effect* of the pay cut is' (personal interview 2016) than take a didactic political line. Focusing on the complexity of human relationships, Zeldin proposes that 'the economics seep into it' (personal interview 2016) in a more understated manner. Ian's sexism and casual racism correspond with his individualistic arrogance and assertion of power, but they also register dramatically as a form of defensive unhappiness with his own situation. Phil's depression and distress compel him periodically to seek refuge in the toilets, while Ian yells threats of non-payment of wages through the wall. These elements of context and character subtly allude to the gendered and racialized aspects of insecure work, and its emotional consequences; the pace of the piece formally reflects the distance between the rhetoric of 'flexibility' and abrasive lived realities.

Zeldin describes the 'heartbeat' of *Beyond Caring* as 'the contact between the inner sensation of an actor, and the person they're meeting' (personal interview 2016) in the research process – a sympathetic encounter that finds its way into the rehearsal room, and thereby into the work itself. Thus, as well as drawing on published accounts, Zeldin spent some time working as a night cleaner himself. Additionally, as Zeldin and actor Janet Etuk explained to me, the company met with workers, campaigners and union activists, who described to them conditions beset with inadequate equipment, insufficient time to complete the work required, and very little recourse. Though *Beyond Caring* is a fiction, in its methods we can see parallels with documentary theatre research and development based on actors' re-enactment (Merlin 2007: 41). It must be emphasized that Zeldin is the author of his works, but the mode of each piece's development is a 'porous process'; and, as he puts it, 'it's not just about actors. The core creativity in every new production comes from the selves of the people that I'm working with' (personal interview 2016). This is a very striking conceptual statement regarding the process of artistic research with people from other walks of life, theatrical mediation of experience, and the relationship between the material conditions of life and human subjectivity. It refuses an idea of acting as solely a form of technical artifice and proposes that creative practice and human subjectivity are entwined. In this understanding, theatre is one manifestation of human action in a larger life-world and is not cordoned off from it.

Similarly, *Beyond Caring*'s scenography conceives of the industrial spaces of the theatre and the factory as inter-articulated. One constructed space, the factory, seamlessly becomes another, the theatre foyer. In its naturalism, the production implicitly proposes that it permits theatrical access to a workplace that would otherwise be inaccessible to most of us. Bathed in light along with the performers, audiences are actively implicated in the social situation that *Beyond Caring* represents: as Zeldin insists, 'there is nowhere to hide' (personal interview 2016). In this scenario, theatre is not a place of fantasy or escape. Subverting what Brecht called the 'culinary' theatre of consumerism, it also departs from a mode of naturalism whereby quasi-absent audience members gaze voyeuristically upon a private space through a 'fourth wall'. In this sense, *Beyond Caring* offers a kind of meta-theatrical commentary on normative conditions of theatrical representation and reception – and in its fragmentary dramaturgy and naturalistic aesthetic, as critic Andrew Haydon suggests, 'there's so much more than "naturalism" at work in the piece. Really, it's more of a meditation than a play' (*Postcards from the Gods* 2016). It does not employ a Brechtian mode of distantiation exactly, but it does challenge its audience to encounter the onstage situation reflexively.

And audiences reacted to that situation in a range of ways. During break times, as the workers are seated around the table, Phil reads Dick Francis's thriller *Blood Sport* (1967), which becomes the object of stilted conversation. In the second of these moments, about a third of the way through the piece, Grace (Janet Etuk) tentatively asks Phil (James Doherty [at HOME]) what is happening in the story. He explains, but not in detail. A silence falls. After a very lengthy pause, she asks him again: 'What's happening now?' (Zeldin 2015: 24). It is as if the story that Phil is reading silently is taking place with them in real time. He offers another brief summary. Then she sidles over slightly, and subtly tries to look at the book. He tilts the book, just as subtly, almost as if he isn't really doing it, so that she can see. At the performance I saw at HOME in Manchester, this moment of offering, of friendship forming, prompted a spontaneous 'ohhh!' of delight in the audience. This instance of generosity contrasts strongly with the miserable performance review Ian (Luke Clarke) conducts with Susan (Kristin Hutchinson) in the penultimate scene of the play, inspired by a questionnaire Southwood discusses in *Non-Stop Inertia* (personal interview 2016). His patronizing observations of her work and brusque tone elicited a loud 'pffffffffffft' from more than one audience member that evening at the National Theatre. And, returning to HOME, the end of that performance witnessed one of the most extraordinary moments I've seen in the theatre. During the curtain call, following the performance's merciless concluding moment of frenzied cleaning, a woman on the front row a few seats down from me stood up and approached Etuk. As the applause tailed off and the other actors began to leave the stage, the audience member held Etuk's hand and earnestly affirmed that her performance of the arthritic seizure truly reflected her own experience.

The production also engendered anger. Zeldin and Etuk describe audience members in Sheffield shouting out during the show:

AZ This is shit.

JE This isn't theatre.

LO What?!

JE This is an observation. This doesn't happen in this country any more.

AZ This is not British. Britain's got labour laws, this couldn't happen.

Personal interview 2016

Following another performance at the National Theatre, a dissatisfied audience member confronted Etuk: 'he found me and tapped me on the back afterwards, just said "rubbish" and walked off' (personal interview 2016). The strength of these responses speaks to the performative workings of the production – the precision of its realism, its disruption of theatre-as-entertainment, and its representation of experiences to which some might respond with ambivalence or agitation in the deeply embattled, unequal context of austerity. They resonate with Erin Hurley's gloss of psychologist William James: emotion is 'inevitably influenced by a person's expectations and interpretative lens; the shape of the expectations and the curvature of the lens are forged in experience and cultural norms that vary across geography and period' (Hurley 2010: 19). The expectations in these examples relate to the clash between assumptions regarding workplace protections and the lived contemporary realities represented in the performance, and between notions of what does and does not count as 'good' or 'legitimate' theatre. These aspects again are intrinsically linked to the relationship between theatre and economic system. Questions of class and income disparity are unavoidably raised by a performance that sensitively represented lives encumbered by poverty, but which itself cost the equivalent of two hours minimum-waged work in the UK to attend, and substantially more in the United States – a barrier addressed in Chicago with the offer of free tickets to temporary workers (Vitali 2017).

Past and present

As I was preparing this chapter, I discussed *Beyond Caring* with a friend who had not seen the production. She made a valuable observation: that it was noteworthy that the piece concerned itself with a factory, and not with digital culture, 'immaterial labour' or other forms of work engaged with telecommunications and the management of information. In this sense, the piece represents a kind of refusal of one narrative about the transformation of work in the rich Western world. Manufacturing jobs as a proportion of economic activity have diminished substantially since the 1970s (Berry 2016). But manual labour, and exploitation based not on wireless connectivity's blurring of work and leisure time but on highly systematized, low- paid, insecure work are lived daily realities. Although consumers may experience online communications and commerce as weightless and instantaneous, back-breaking assiduously timetabled work at 'fulfilment centres' for global organizations like Amazon still facilitates the provision of goods in a service economy, as investigative reporting attests (Cadwalladr 2013). Aditya Chakrabortty writes that the rare example of *Beyond Caring* demonstrates 'how poorly the theatre and the arts more broadly have handled the crisis', congratulating the piece 'for putting down the microscope and picking up the widescreen lens' (Chakrabortty 2015: 33) – that is, for departing from narratives about powerful executives, and paying attention to the wider context of insecure work and its environments.

The cinematic metaphor of 'widescreen lens' seems an unusual one, but is apt for *Beyond Caring*'s painstaking realism, and reflects the uptake of tropes of the screen in other criticism. Time and again critics drew attention to the piece's naturalism – speaking of its 'rare quality of gripping authenticity' (Cavendish 2015), the performative details 'so faultlessly convincing that you almost feel you are spying via CCTV' (Marlowe 2015), its 'unostentatious naturalism' (Hemming 2015), and its 'Mike Leigh-esque social realism with pinches of heightened theatricality' (Anon 2015). While close attention to visual detail is a time-honoured realist strategy, its uncompromising use of lengthy silence made the piece feel to me to be bold and newly experimental. And strangely, its experimentalism resonated with Martin Esslin's thoughts, written in 1968, on the emergence of naturalism in the nineteenth century and its subsequent development. Esslin proposed then that nineteenth-century naturalism, 'an iconoclastic, revolutionary onslaught against the establishment has now turned into the embodiment of "squareness", conservatism and the contemporary concept of the well-made play' (Esslin 1968: 67). Both these perceptions of naturalism, and the proximity between 'sign-vehicle and content' (States 1985: 20) in theatrical representation might also account for critical hostility to non-naturalistic approaches to economic questions. For example, Caroline Horton's *Islands* (2015), a magnificently scatological *buffon*

Figure 2   *Beyond Caring*. Victoria Moseley, Sean O'Callaghan, Hayley Carmichael, Janet Etuk. Photo: Mark Douet.

treatment of tax havens, alienated several critics, who felt that the economic content and clownish form of the piece were mismatched (for example, Billington 2015).

For me, like *Islands*, *Beyond Caring* succeeded brilliantly in producing apt '*feeling*' (*Postcards from the Gods* 2015) – in this case, desolation, joy, hope and anger befitting the situation on stage. And *Beyond Caring*'s naturalistic representations were the precise opposite of jaded aesthetic conservatism, nonetheless echoing critical images from nineteenth-century theatre. Gazing upon *Beyond Caring*'s factory for the first time, I thought more and more of the boots resting in the kitchen in Strindberg's *Miss Julie* (1888), and the portrait of Hedda Gabler's father in Ibsen's 1891 play, hanging portentously in the background – symbols of profoundly effective patriarchal dominance and hierarchy. The equivalent in *Beyond Caring* of these absent-but-present fathers is the unseen boss Richard, whom Ian toadyingly mentions has lately celebrated his marriage with a big white wedding. While in *Miss Julie*, the revelation of private sex sabotages public respectability, in the interaction between Phil and Becky, we see sex pushed from home into work, with no reputational consequences but profound psychic ones. As a title, *Beyond Caring* evokes the abandonment of the state and the characters' ensuing forced abandonment of their own children, as well as the emotional extremity of the situation, which Chakrabortty characterizes as an 'acid bath' (Chakrabortty 2015). Raymond Williams argues that in naturalism, 'environments are integral parts of the dramatic action, indeed, in a true sense, are themselves actors and agencies' (Williams [1980] 1997: 128). We can absolutely see that principle reflected in *Beyond Caring*, and also, with its lighting decisions, a dramaturgical critique, where 'action is seen not only within an environment but as itself, within certain limits and pressures, producing an environment' (127). In his discussion of nineteenth-century naturalism in England, Williams asks after 'the relations between forms and social formations' (147). Despite their many differences, the dramaturgical affinity between *Beyond Caring* and much earlier socially critical plays suggests a strong connection between the socioeconomic and industrial conditions of the late-nineteenth century and the early twenty-first.

Performance details

The Pajama Game: A Musical Comedy, premiere St James Theatre, New York 1954, music and lyrics by Richard Adler and Jerry Ross, book by George Abbott and Richard Bissell, directed by George Abbott and Jerome Robbins. For more information, see 'The Pajama Game' broadwaymusicalhome.com/shows/pajama.htm (accessed March 2018).

Beyond Caring, premiere Yard Theatre, London 2014, written and directed by Alexander Zeldin, designer: Natasha Jenkins, sound designer: Josh Anio Grigg, lighting designer: Marc Williams, assistant director: Grace Gummer. With Sean O'Callaghan (Phil), Luke Clarke (Ian), Victoria Mosley (Becky), Hayley Carmichael (Susan) and Janet Etuk (Grace). In subsequent productions in Britain, the roles of Susan and Phil were performed by Kristin Hutchinson and James Edward Doherty.

These interviews with Alexander Zeldin provide great insights into the research and development process:

Catherine Love, 'Alexander Zeldin: "The Director as God is Bullshit"', *Exeunt Magazine*, 21 April 2015. Available online: http://exeuntmagazine.com/features/the-director-as-god-is-bullshit/ (accessed January 2018).

'Director Alexander Zeldin talks Beyond Caring', *HomeMCR*, 12 July 2016. Available online: https://homemcr.org/article/director-alexander-zeldin-talks-beyond-caring (accessed January 2018).

Max McGuinness, 'Playwright Alexander Zeldin on the power – and limitations – of theatre', *Financial Times*, 29 March 2017, Available online: https://www.ft.com/content/48303ffe-13d4-11e7-b0c1-37e417ee6c76 (accessed January 2018).

And this review of *Beyond Caring* in Chicago and video interview with Alexander Zeldin and David Schwimmer (Lookingglass Theatre co-founder) offer fascinating comparison and contrast between the European and North American contexts:

Chris Jones, 'Review: "Beyond Caring" is about the work, done right in your face', *Chicago Tribune*, 2 April 2018. Available online: http://www.chicagotribune.com/entertainment/theater/reviews/ct-beyond-caring-review-ent-0403-20170402-column.html (accessed January 2018).

Marc Vitali, 'David Schwimmer on "Beyond Caring" at Lookingglass', *Chicago Tonight*, 5 April 2017. Available online: http://chicagotonight.wttw.com/2017/04/05/david-schwimmer-beyond-caring-lookingglass (accessed January 2018).

Further Reading

For a close reading and contextualization of Marx's *Capital, Volume 1*, see Harvey (2010 and 2008–17). David Harvey's lectures on *Capital, Volume 2* and *Marx and Capital* can also be accessed at his website. For an analysis of the intersection between sexual identity and capitalism from a materialist feminist standpoint, see Hennessy (2000). For an account of the class politics of the theatre industry and representations of poverty on stage, see Gardner (2016). And for a contextualization of zero hours contracts departing from a visit to *Beyond Caring*, see Mason (2014).

References

Abbott, George, and Richard Bissell (1954), *The Pajama Game*, London: Warner Chappell Music.

Allain, Paul, and Jen Harvie (2006), *The Routledge Companion to Theatre and Performance*, Abingdon and New York: Routledge.

Anon (2018), 'The Pajama Game'. Available online: http://broadwaymusicalhome.com/shows/pajama.htm (accessed March 2018).

Anon (2015), 'Also Showing', *The Sunday Times*, 10 May.

Athanasiou, Athena (2011), 'Becoming Precarious through Regimes of Gender, Capital, and Nation', *Hot Spots: Cultural Anthropology*, 28 October. Available online: https://culanth.org/fieldsights/250-becoming-precarious-through-regimes-of-gender-capital-and-nation (accessed January 2018).

Aubernas, Florence ([2010] 2011), *The Night Cleaner*, Cambridge and Malden, MA: Polity Press.

Bell, David, and David Blanchflower (2013), 'Underemployment in the UK Revisited', *National Institute Economic Review*, 229: F8–F22. Available online: https://www.dartmouth.edu/~blnchflr/papers/bell&blanchflower2013.pdf (accessed January 2018).

Berry, Craig (2016), 'SPERI British Political Economy Brief No. 25: UK Manufacturing Decline Since the Crisis in Historical Perspective', *Sheffield Political Economy Research Institute*, October. Available online: http://speri.dept.shef.ac.uk/wp-content/uploads/2016/10/Brief-25-UK-manufacturing-decline-since-the-crisis.pdf (accessed January 2018).

'Beyond Caring – HOME, Manchester [seen 14/07/16]', *Postcards from the Gods*, 16 July 2016. Available online: https://postcardsgods.blogspot.co.uk/2016/07/beyond-caring-home-manchester.html (accessed January 2018).

Blyth, Mark (2013), 'The Austerity Delusion: Why a Bad Idea Won Over the West', *Foreign Affairs*, May/June: 41–56.

Borda, Jennifer L. (2010) 'Working-class Women, Protofeminist Performance, and Resistant Ruptures in the Movie Musical The Pajama Game', *Text and Performance Quarterly*, 30 (3): 227–46.

Brecht, Bertolt (2001), *Brecht on Theatre: The Development of an Aesthetic*, ed. and trans. J. Willett, London: Methuen.

Brown, Wendy (2015), *Undoing the Demos: Neoliberalism's Stealth Revolution*, New York: Zone Books.

Cadwalladr, Carol (2013) 'My Week as an Amazon Insider', *The Observer*, 1 December.

Cavendish, Dominic (2015), '*Beyond Caring*, National Theatre, Review: "Gripping Authenticity"', *Daily Telegraph*, 3 May.

Chakrabortty, Aditya (2015), 'In Praise of . . . Beyond Caring', *The Guardian*, 15 May: 33.

'economy, n.', OED Online, *Oxford University Press*. Available online: http://0-www.oed.com. catalogue.libraries.london.ac.uk/view/Entry/59393 (accessed January 2018).

Esslin, Martin (1968), 'Naturalism in Context', *TDR: The Drama Review*, 13 (2): 67–76.

Federici, Silvia (2012), *Revolution at Point Zero: Housework, Reproduction, and Feminist Struggle*, Oakland: PM Press.

Fine, Ben, and Alfredo Saad-Filho (2004), *Marx's Capital*, 4th edition, London and Ann Arbor: Pluto Press.

Gardner, Lyn (2016) '"Poverty Porn": How Middle-Class Theatres Depict Britain's Poor', *The Guardian: Theatre Blog*, 15 April. Available online: https://www.theguardian.com/stage/theatreblog/2016/apr/15/poverty-porn-theatre-boy-yen-rehome (accessed January 2018).

Goldhill, Simon (1997), 'The Audience of Athenian Tragedy', in P. E. Easterling (ed.), *The Cambridge Companion to Greek Tragedy*, 54–68, Cambridge: Cambridge University Press.

Harvey, David (2010), *A Companion to Marx's Capital*, London and New York: Verso.

Harvey, David (1990), *The Condition of Postmodernity: An Enquiry into the Origins of Cultural Change*, Oxford: Blackwell.

Harvey, David (2008–17) 'Reading Capital with David Harvey', *DavidHarvey.org*. Available online: http://davidharvey.org/reading-capital/ (accessed January 2018).

Hemming, Sarah (2015) 'Beyond Caring, National Theatre, London – Review', *Financial Times*, 5 May.

Hennessy, Rosemary (2000), *Profit and Pleasure: Sexual Identities in Late Capitalism*, New York and London: Routledge.

Herod, Andrew, and Luis L. M. Aguiar (2016), 'Introduction: Cleaners and the Dirty Work of Neoliberalism', *Antipode*, 38 (3): 425–34.

Hobsbawm, Eric (1969), *Industry and Empire*, London: Pelican.

Hurley, Erin (2010), *Theatre and Feeling*, Basingstoke: Palgrave Macmillan.

Inman, Philip (2015), 'Almost 700,000 People in UK Have Zero-hours Contract as Main Job', *The Guardian*, 25 February. Available online: https://www.theguardian.com/uk-news/2015/feb/25/zero-hours-contract-rise-staff-figures (accessed January 2018).

Joseph, Miranda (2002), *Against the Romance of Community*, Minneapolis: University of Minnesota Press.

King, Pamela M. (2006), *The York Mystery Cycle and the Worship of the City*, Cambridge: D. S. Brewer.

Knowles, Ric (2004), *Reading the Material Theatre*, Cambridge: Cambridge University Press.

Labour Party (2015), 'The Labour Party Manifesto 2015'. Available online: http://action.labour.org.uk/page/-/A4#20BIG#c20_PRINT_ENG_LABOUR#20MANIFESTO_TEXT#20LAYOUT.pdf (accessed January 2018).

Marlowe, Sam (2015), 'Beyond Caring, NT Temporary', *The Times*, 5 May.

Marx, Karl ([1867] 1990), *Capital: A Critique of Political Economy, Volume One*, trans. B. Fowkes, London: Penguin.

Mason, Paul (2014) 'There Are no Heroes on the Zero-Hours Borderline', *Channel 4 News*, 11 July. Available online: https://www.channel4.com/news/by/paul-mason/blogs/heroes-zerohours-borderline (accessed January 2018).

Meiksins Wood, Ellen ([1999] 2002), *The Origin of Capitalism: A Longer View*, London: Verso.

Merlin, Bella (2007), '*The Permanent Way* and the Impermanent Muse', *Contemporary Theatre Review*, 17 (1): 41–9.

Monaghan, Angela (2017), 'Record 910,000 UK Workers on Zero-Hours Contracts', *The Guardian*, 3 March. Available online: https://www.theguardian.com/business/2017/mar/03/zero-hours-contracts-uk-record-high (accessed January 2018).

Personal interview with Alexander Zeldin and Janet Etuk, September 2016.

Postcards from the Gods (2015), 'Islands – Bush Theatre', 24 January. Available online: https://postcardsgods.blogspot.co.uk/2015/01/islands-bush-theatre.html (accessed January 2018).

Pyper, Doug, and Jennifer Brown (2016), *House of Commons Library: Briefing Paper Number 06553, 13 April 2016: Zero-hours contracts*. Available online: http://researchbriefings.parliament.uk/ResearchBriefing/Summary/SN06553 (accessed January 2018).

Ridout, Nicholas (2006), *Stage Fright, Animals and Other Theatrical Problems*, Cambridge: Cambridge University Press.

Southwood, Ivor (2011), *Non-Stop Inertia*, Winchester and Washington: Zero Books.

States, Bert O. (1985), *Great Reckonings in Little Rooms: On the Phenomenology of Theatre*, Berkeley and Los Angeles: University of California Press.

Vitali, Marc (2017), 'David Schwimmer on "Beyond Caring" at Lookingglass', *Chicago Tonight*, 5 April. Available online: http://chicagotonight.wttw.com/2017/04/05/david-schwimmer-beyond-caring-lookingglass (accessed January 2018).

Wa Thiong'o, Ngugi (1986), *Decolonising the Mind: The Politics of Language in African Literature*, London: James Currey.

Willett, John (1977), *The Theatre of Bertolt Brecht*, London: Methuen Drama.

Williams, Raymond ([1980] 1997), *Problems in Materialism and Culture*, London and New York: Verso.

Williams, Simon (1994), 'Ibsen and the Theatre, 1877–1900', in James McFarlane (ed.), *The Cambridge Companion to Ibsen*, 165–82, Cambridge: Cambridge University Press.

Zeldin, Alexander (2015), *Beyond Caring*, London: Bloomsbury.

Beyond Caring

Beyond Caring received its world premiere at The Yard Theatre, London, on 1 July 2014, directed by Alexander Zeldin, with the following cast and creative team:

Susan	Hayley Carmichael
Ian	Luke Clarke
Grace	Janet Etuk
Becky	Victoria Moseley
Phil	Sean O'Callaghan

Set and Costume Designer	Natasha Jenkins
Sound Designer	Josh Grigg
Lighting Designer	Marc Williams
Assistant Director	Grace Gummer

It subsequently transferred to the National Theatre's Temporary Space where it opened on 28 April 2015 with the following cast:

Ian	Luke Clarke
Grace	Janet Etuk
Susan	Kristin Hutchinson
Becky	Victoria Moseley
Phil	Sean O'Callaghan

Beyond Caring received its European premiere at Théâtre de la Ville de Luxembourg on 16 June 2016 with the following cast:

Ian	Luke Clarke
Phil	Paddy Doherty
Grace	Janet Etuk
Susan	Kristin Hutchinson
Becky	Victoria Moseley

Notes

'.' marks a thought that doesn't become a word.

/ marks an interruption that means the actors speak over one another.

There are a lot of long silences, that can be drawn out.

The entire action takes place in a small loading bay area just inside a meat factory somewhere on the edges of a city in the western world. Due to refurbishment the place has been made into a makeshift break-room for the day staff.

There is a foldable table, a coffee area with a machine in one corner. Roll cages and boxes in the other. The wall is dirty and will never get clean. A toilet is in the corner. A fire-door opens up to the outside of the space, which is periodically opened so we can see the outside. The entire space is lit throughout the piece, including the seating area where the audience are. It is preferable to use non-theatrical lighting, such as fluorescent strip lights.

Phil, *fifty, thirty hours a week.*
Ian, *twenty-seven, full time.*
Becky, *thirty-six, agency worker.*
Susan, *forty-eight, agency worker*
Grace, *twenty-seven, agency worker*

The play contains a few quotes from Dick Francis's novel Blood Sport. *The material isn't quoted directly in this script, so if you're performing the play, we suggest you obtain a copy of this edition to reference the quotes directly.*

Act One

Scene One

The interview and induction.

Phil *enters.*

A time.

He goes to the loo. Locks the door. A time.

Becky *enters from the outer door – goes to the back wall. A time.*

Susan *enters.*

Becky   You here for the cleaning?

Susan   Yeh.

A time.

Ian *enters, drags a chair to the middle of the space.*

Ian   Morning. Do you wanna grab a seat?

They do, they take the seats to the middle of the space where he is.

Ian   Passports?

They find them and hand them over.

Susan   Birth certificate . . . /

Ian   That's fine.

Right help yourselves to coffee I'm just gonna get these copied.

He exits quickly. A short time.

Susan   Do you want one?

Becky   Oh no thanks . . .

Susan   What's your name?

Becky   Becky.

Susan   Susan.

Short time.

Susan *goes to the coffee machine in the corner. Comes back.*

Susan   You have to pay for it.

A time. Nothing passes between them. **Becky** *is on her phone.*

Ian comes back in. Hands back passports. Sits down, looks at forms.

Ian   Alright, Rebecca.

During the following, **Phil** *comes out of the toilet. Head bowed, he goes to the table. Sits. No acknowledgement. He sits at the table and begins to read a book.*

Becky   Becky.

Ian   Thirty-six.

Becky   Yes.

Ian   Which agency you with, List Recruitment is that right?

Becky *nods.*

Ian   And it says you've had some cleaning experience with estate agents.

Becky   Yeah. I was there for about three weeks.

Ian   OK. Which makes you . . . Susan? List too?

Susan   Sorry?

Ian   List Recruitment?

Susan   Yes.

Loud knock on the door.

Ian   Yeh come in.

Susan   I'm forty-eight

Ian   . . . Good.

Grace *enters from side door. She has a limp. She leaves the door open.*

Grace   Is this for, um, cleaning?

Ian   Yeah.

Grace   OK.

She goes back to the door, to close it this time.

Ian's *hand is outstretched (for the passport).* **Grace** *offers her hand to him to shake it.*

Grace   Oh hi I'm Grace /

Ian   No, I want your passport . . .

He takes the passport.

He exits to copy the passport.

Grace   Sorry . . . I'm not usually this . . . late.

Phil *brings a chair over for her. Lined up with the other three facing* **Ian**'*s vacant seat.*

Grace   Thank you!

Phil   .

Susan   There's coffee.

Grace   No I'm alright thank you.

She puts on some make-up – the others watch her as she does this. She's come in her best clothes for the interview.

A time.

Ian *returns.*

Grace   Sorry, what, what was your name?

Ian   Ian.

Grace   Ian, my agency only called me about this this morning so they said they would call you to say / I'd be a few minutes late.

Ian   Yeh I didn't get the call.

He looks over her papers.

Ian   Right, Grace.

Grace   Yes, yeh.

Ian   Twenty-seven.

Grace   Yes.

Ian   Same age as me.

Grace   Great.

Ian   When's your birthday?

Grace   February the eleventh.

Ian   .

He reads.

It says something here about disability, benefits . . .

Grace   Yeah I was exempt from work but I went to an assessment /

Ian   Do you mind me asking what's wrong with / you

Grace   Rheumatoid arthritis.

Ian   But you've /

Grace   Yes I've been cleared for work.

Ian   That's fine /

Grace   That's fine.

So it just, erm I was exempt but I went to an assessment I have my form here.

She walks over to him with the form that she has taken from her bag.

There's just this bit at the top /

Ian   Yep I've seen one before. /

Grace   And then at the bottom there's the con /

Ian   No I'm not saying anything /

Grace   Yeh no /

Ian   Obviously you're going to have to keep up.

Reading.

What's the medication break?

Grace   Oh I take it with food . . . so.

Ian   And no heavy lifting. (*Under his breath.*) Great.

OK well you'll potentially be doing here is every night both cleaning this room on a regular basis – we are going through a refurb at the minute – so there's a temporary lack of space so this area – the loading area – is now the temporary break room for the day staff as you can see but also in that area there is coffee for us. As well as that we need to clean all the other communal areas of the factory, three sets of toilets, the dry stores and the offices.

Becky   Excuse me, when do we find out what shifts we're doing?

Ian   As your agencies will have told you, this is a fourteen consecutive day position. But I can't tell you what or how many hours you're going to be working as responsiveness is part of the brief.

Susan   Pay is on Friday right?

Ian   Maybe I think so – speak to your agencies.

So some of the cleaning equipment you'll be familiar with, we use mops, brushes, brooms, that sort of thing. That's Phil by the way.

Phil   Hi.

Beat.

Ian   And some of the equipment is a bit more specialised, I'll just demonstrate that now.

Wheels over the floor buffer – it is huge and on four wheels, battery operated.

This, the shampoolux 4000 . . . or as Phil and I call it, 'the beast'. We call it 'the beast' don't we, Phil?

Phil   Yeh, 'the beast'.

Ian   Why do we call it 'the beast'? Cos you've got to tame it, yeah, control it. Get it to listen to you.

Becky are you listening?

Becky   Yeh.

Ian   Because if you're not listening you won't understand – this is a very serious piece of equipment. You can easily let it run away from you causing injury to you or others. You could cause real damage to the building. Structural damage or . . . other damage.

So just a quick demonstration, straight on with the key, push the button that says brushes and then . . .

The beast is on, it makes a very loud noise.

Squeezing the triggers forward you're looking for a nice sweeping motion.

He demonstrates.

A nice sweeping motion.

Proceeding at a steady pace.

He turns the beast off.

A short time.

OK who wants to go first?

Beat.

Susan   I don't think I can manage that.

Ian   Right well you'll have to so . . .

A short time.

Becky   I've got a driving licence do you think that'll help?

Ian   Great OK.

Right so just hold there and there and . . .

Becky *does it. It doesn't go well but she just about keeps hold of it.*

Ian   Good, well done.

Susan.

Susan   .

Ian   Hold there and there.

Do you want me to turn it on for you?

Susan *is very stiff with it and doesn't know how to use it too well either. She leaves it still running when she returns to her chair.*

Ian   Grace.

Grace *has a go as well. It is too heavy for her and she has an accident. Running into* **Ian***'s chair.*

Ian   Stop stop it stop it.

OK OK OK it's OK. Alright.

OK thank you for that.

Grace *is still holding on to the beast.*

It's fine.

She moves away.

Jesus Christ.

A short time.

Phil, can you put this away, please.

Can you all put your chairs away.

A time.

OK. You'll get a text from your agencies saying what time to come in tonight.

Becky   Tonight?

Susan   All of us?

Ian   Tonight, yeah, it'll be from nine to two.

Do you want to grab your heavy lifting training on the way out – read it and tick the right box to show you've understood.

He hands them a photocopy of an instructive diagram on how to lift heavy objects.

Susan   Thank you.

They all say bye – improvised.

Phil *marks the page in his book and exits.*

Grace *is left alone on stage.*

She redoes the scene in her head . . . Goes to get her stuff but tarries a minute.

She discreetly goes to the beast on her own, tries to get the beast to work, slowly, surely. She struggles. It is very heavy for her. She is muttering under her breath – words we can't make out.

She looks up. Breathes out.

Blackout.

Scene Two

Work scene one. Night shift.

They are cleaning the room sweeping, having already cleaned another part of the factory. Everything has been done in a rush – the time allocated isn't sufficient. Grace goes to the beast thinking that this is what she should do now. She turns it on and begins.

Becky   Grace what are you doing we haven't swept here yet.

Susan   You're not meant to use that machine on this floor.

Grace   Sorry.

A long time. Silence. We just watch them sweeping the filthy floor.

Susan   Do you think we could ask them to give us gloves?

Becky   Yeh dunno speak to Ian.

A long time. Silence. Cleaning.

Grace *goes to the break table where she takes a small yellow pouch out of her bag in which she keeps her medicine. She takes some medicine.*

Becky   Have you done them toilets yet, Grace?

Grace *puts the medicine away and runs to the loos.*

Phil *comes in.*

Phil   We're on a break now.

Susan   What?

They wonder whether to take a break as they haven't finished the work. **Susan** *keeps cleaning before taking a break.*

Grace *exits the toilet carrying a bag full of wet paper – the toilet was blocked.*

A short time. Finally they gather round the table.

Break 1.

Grace *is looking at her medicine, measuring up what she needs to take that day and getting a packet of biscuits out.* **Phil** *is reading his book.*

A time.

Susan   It's good to have a break.

Becky   Tell me about it.

Susan   Yeah.

A time.

Grace   I think I had a dream about this place last night.

Becky   What?

Grace   It's just the lights . . . /

Becky *puts on some music on her mobile phone. It plays through the speakers of her phone, loudly. Daft Punk's 'Get Lucky'.*

It plays. A time.

The music is interrupted by a ringtone. She takes a call. Leaves by the side door.

Becky   Hiya, love.

Susan   I was enjoying that.

A time.

She pulls out an old tape recorder from her bag. Rewinds the tape. At first it plays some Spanish lessons but she fast-forwards it. A bad quality recording of 'Bridge Over Troubled Water' by Simon and Garfunkel blares out.

Susan   Is that a bit loud?

Phil   No.

They listen to the music. **Phil** *begins to hum along to this song. Singing a few of the words timidly.* **Susan** *and he share a smile.*

Susan   I've got more cheery songs if you prefer, Phil.

The tape player cuts out. She tries to restart it. Shakes it, plays, stops, plays.

Susan   My battery died.

A short time.

Grace   What's . . .

What. What are you reading, Phil?

Phil   Dick Francis – *Blood Sport.*

Grace   What's it about?

Phil   It's about this private investigator. He's trying to find these horses.

These thoroughbreds that have been kidnapped.

It's really good.

Grace   Yeh?

Phil   Yeh. I've read all his stuff. 'Against all Odds', 'Bonecrack', 'The Edge'.

It's really good.

Have you read any of his stuff?

Grace   No. I'm not a good reader. God help me . . .

Susan   Do you like horse riding?

He was a jockey, Dick Francis, wasn't he? /

Becky *has come back in with a thought – it's a shift in rhythm.*

Becky   Excuse me.

Pause.

Excuse me.

Yeh you.

What's your name?

Phil   Phil.

Becky   Nice to meet you yeh. You work here full time don't you? /

Phil   Yeh /

Becky   Who do I need to talk to about getting a day off?

Phil   Uh I don't know. Ian I suppose.

Becky   Is Ian the boss?

Phil   No Richard's the boss. He's in charge of the night. Shift. /

Ian *has come in – silence suddenly.*

A short time. **Ian** *wanders over to* **Becky** *who is back in her phone.*

Ian   Was that Daft Punk you were listening to earlier?

Becky   Yeh.

Ian   Have you heard the Kanye remix?

Susan (*simultaneous to* **Grace**)   Where are they from? (*About the biscuits on the table.*)

Becky (*to* **Ian**)   Nah.

Grace   Lidl.

Susan   .

Grace   They're 20p cheaper than Tesco at the moment, you can get a coupon in the *Metro* for them.

A short time. There are some newspapers on the table. **Susan** *half-heartedly looks through them very quickly.*

Grace   Do you want one?

Susan   No. You're alright.

Short time.

Go on yeh.

She takes half the packet, when **Grace** *isn't looking. And puts them into her bag.*

She takes half of one and eats a bit of it.

A time.

Ian *looks at his watch, wanders down the stage to be in full view of all of them.*

Ian (*looks at his watch counting down the seconds*) Back to work.

He waits for them all to leave.

Becky *has lingered. She turns to* **Ian**.

Becky   Ian.

Ian   Yeah.

Becky   You're like the boss right?

Ian   Yeah.

Becky   So is it you I talk to about getting a day off?

Ian   It's a fourteen day contract so /

Becky   I know but I wouldn't ask if it wasn't important. I just need this Saturday /

Ian   OK yeh I'll see what I can do but

Becky   I appreciate it thank you /

Ian   I'm not making any promises but I'll speak to Richard.

Becky   Yeh, no thank you.

Ian *stares at her arse intently as she walks out.*

He goes over to the table where **Grace** *and others have left bags. He briefly looks through them.*

He goes to sit at the table and does nothing. Stares vacantly into space.

A quite long time

Blackout.

Scene Three

Work scene 2 – another night soon after.

They are all mopping the floor. **Phil** *is cleaning the back wall. They all have gloves now, apart from* **Susan** *who only has one.* **Susan** *and* **Becky** *are mopping with wheeled mop buckets.* **Susan**'s *bucket is on only three wheels – one of the wheels is broken. The buckets both make a noise as they are rolled.*

Grace *bends down to something she's seen on the floor. She's found a bracelet. She picks it up, it sparkles.*

Grace   Ian?

Ian   Yeh.

Grace   I've found a bracelet.

Ian *looks at it.*

Grace   If no one wants it I'll have it.

Ian   I'll put it in lost property.

Grace   Yeh of course.

Ian   Oh you're doing the boxes today.

Grace *stands centre stage. Waiting.*

A time. **Susan** *is mopping upstage towards her.*

Susan   Shove up, Grace.

Ian *comes back in with plastic boxes. They have two plastic bags in them full of animal liquid fat.*

Ian   Take them out before you clean them.

Grace *tries to lift one but some of the fat spills on the boxes and the floor.*

Ian   Jesus Christ! Leave it /

Grace   It's fine . . . /

Ian   Leave it.

He takes it outside.

That is not my job.

Can you just clean them please.

Grace   Yep.

A time. **Grace** *cleans. She stops after a moment and goes and takes some pills from her bag by the table.* **Susan** *goes to change the water in her mop bucket offstage.*

Becky *is, intermittently, looking at* **Phil** *who is cleaning the back wall.*

Becky   How long you been here then, Phil?

Phil   Couple of years.

Becky   What did you do before?

Phil   I was a nursing auxiliary.

Becky   What's one of them?

Phil   It's like a nurse but without the qualifications.

Becky   So like not really a nurse then?

Short time.

She squeezes the water out of her mop and begins to mop again.

Becky   So how come you left that job for this?

Phil   Me wife . . . it's a long story.

Susan *comes in with a new bucket full – it makes noise.* **Phil** *stands still for a moment, back to the audience, and then goes towards the toilet.*

Susan   Have you seen my other glove?

Becky   No.

A short time.

Grace   Have you noticed that the price has gone up on the coffee . . . it was only like 40p before.

Susan   It's gone up 20 pence then, that's a bit much.

Grace   Yeah and the change, they don't give it to you . . . I put a pound in.

A time.

Becky   It must have been alright living on them benefits before they cut you off.

Grace   Yeh it helped me a fair bit.

Becky   How much you get a week?

Grace   It was enough.

They cut me off . . . said I have to work.

Becky   Too bad. I think I'm just gonna fuck it all off and go back on benefits myself.

Grace   Yeh. (*Laughing.*)

Beat.

Still it's alright this as a place to work isn't it / as far as they go /

Becky   You got to be fucking joking it's a cave.

Grace   Yeh, no.

Becky *moves away. Short time.* **Susan** *is swearing under her voice.*

Susan   Bloody bloody.

Becky   You alright Susan /

Susan   I'VE ONLY GOT THREE WHEELS ON MY BLOODY THING.

A short time.

Becky   Hot.

She takes off her coat and jumper; she's wearing a vest now.

Grace   I think you're going to go on to things Becky – I can see you on TV or something like a weather woman or something . . .

Becky   What the fuck are you talking about?

Grace   I'm just saying you look nice.

Becky   Whatever.

Short time.

Where's Phil?

Grace   I don't know.

Becky   .

Long time – they clean.

Susan   Where is it? Where is it?

Audible now, quite worried about it.

Did anyone see my other glove?

Becky   NO, SUSAN, I haven't seen it.

Susan   It must be here somewhere, it must be. I've been looking for it all morning. I told myself that it must be here, because it's not in there, and if it's not in there, then it must be in here.

She looks around for it.

Ian *enters.*

Ian   What spray is that?

Grace   It's, it's for the contaminates . . .

Ian   No it's not. The one for the contaminates has a red band here.

Go and get it.

Grace *goes to get the other spray.*

Ian   Repeat it to yourself, red for contaminates.

Grace   Red for contaminates . . .

Coming back.

You know we could maybe keep the sprays over the other side /

Ian   We'll keep the sprays where I say we keep the sprays.

Grace   No, just because it'd be easier /

Ian   It'd be easier if you carried on with what you were meant to be doing /

Grace   Yeh. No.

I usually get it right /

Ian   Well you got it wrong.

Grace   Yeh / No /

Ian   Right /

Grace   Yeh I'm not saying

Ian   Well you know . . .

Grace   .

She cleans with the right spray.

Grace   Ian I was wondering.

Are there any more shifts this week? /

Ian   Where's Phil?

Grace   I don't know

Susan   I think he's in the loo

Ian   OK right. How long has he been in there for?

Becky   Twenty minutes!

Beat.

Ian   OK, he does this sometimes. Leave it to me.

He goes to the door of the toilet. Looks around. They are all staring at him.

Just give me some space

He speaks into the door.

Ian   Phil?

Phil! You coming out mate?

Beat.

You alright in there, Phil?

Beat.

I know we all get down sometimes, yeh, but let's crack on. Do you want to come out and talk it just me and you? Phil?

Silence.

They said you been in there fifteen minutes so . . . time to come out yeh?

Phil   I'll be out in a minute /

Ian   No, Phil, not in a minute, Phil, now please.

Beat.

Right come on out.

Phil   I'll be out in a minute . . .

Ian   Right, I'm NOT PAYING YOU for those twenty minutes you've been in there. Do you understand that? Phil?

Phil   Ian I'm /

Ian   Right we're having lunch. What d'you want? Fifteen minutes or half an hour?

Silence.

I SWEAR TO GOD, PHIL, FIFTEEN MINUTES OR HALF AN HOUR?

Silence.

FIFTEEN MINUTES OR HALF AN HOUR?

Phil   Fifteen minutes.

Ian   Right fifteen minutes.

You are NOT getting paid for those twenty. OK?

To all the others.

Right that's lunch what do you want?

Grace   Fifteen.

Becky   Fifteen yeh.

Susan   Fifteen minutes.

Ian *exits.*

Break 2.

A moment: they all, silently, take off their tabards and go to get their bags to have their packed lunch. **Grace** *left alone.*

She goes towards the door.

She knocks on the door

Grace   You alright in there?

The other two have come back in now. They stand in silence and watch.

Phil   Is that you, Grace?

Grace   Yes.

Do you want to come out?

Phil   .

Grace   It's alright I mean you can stay in there . . . I was just checking.

A short time. They are all settled. **Becky** *is eating a packet of crisps.*

Susan *hasn't got any lunch.*

Phil *comes out. Stands immobile for a minute.*

Phil   Sorry.

Everyone looks at him. He makes his way to the table.

A time. Silence.

Susan   Good to get a break.

Becky   Tell me about it.

A short time. Silence.

Grace   Oh I remembered my dream from the other day I was talking about . . .

She drifts off, perhaps she's forgotten it again.

Susan *stands up, sits down, stands up again.*

Susan   I'm going to treat myself to a mocha choca.

Grace   Don't you have anything to eat?

Susan *goes towards the machine.*

Susan   No no, mocha choca.

Silence again.

Becky   I need a cigarette.

She goes out for a cigarette.

Susan *is at the machine, putting money in and pressing the button. Nothing happens apart from a beeping noise the machine is making but it isn't giving her any coffee.*

Susan   Do you just press it?

Grace   I don't know.

She keeps pressing the button, and the beep is repeated several times, accelerating. Nothing happens.

Susan   I just lost a pound.

Phil   Yeh it always does that.

Grace   It's not right is it?

Susan   NO.

Phil   It does that.

Susan   What?

Phil   Takes your money.

Beat.

Susan *starts to hit the machine, to shake it, trying to get the pound back.*

Nothing happens.

Finally she comes back in. Slowly.

A time.

Grace   How is it? Dick Francis, is it still good?

Phil   Yeah.

Beat.

Grace   What's happening?

Phil   Uh, the private investigator who is investigating, he's gone undercover.

A time. **Grace** *looks upwards, imagining.*

Grace   What's happening now?

Phil   The private investigator's still undercover. But he's in a hotel room now.

Grace *moves closer to try and read the book.*

Grace   I'm not a great reader but you could maybe read out a bit.

Phil   What?

Grace   Well just like where you are? You could maybe read a little bit of /

Phil   I'm not going to read out loud am I? No . . .

Grace   Just like a few sentences or /

Phil   It'll sound stupid! I'm not going to do that.

Grace   We don't have a TV or anything so /

Phil   I'm not going to read out loud I'll sound like an idiot /

Susan   Go on, Phil.

Phil   What? Like read out loud?

Grace   Just a little /

Phil   Yeh? /

Grace   Yeh just a little . . . where you're investigating /

Phil   Yeh? Alright um.

It'll sound stupid though.

Reading from Blood Sport *by Dick Francis:*

Alright . . .

He reads the passage from 'John came out of the bathroom' up to 'Excuyse me', the latter with a forced German accent.

I'm not doing the German accent. I'll sound stupid /

Grace   No it's good.

Phil   No . . . I'll sound like a prat.

Susan   Go on, Phil.

Phil   No . . . /

Grace   Try it /

Phil   No . . .

Grace   It'll be good.

Phil   No . . . what you eating by the way?

Grace   . . . I've just got some biscuits and some cereal . . . /

Phil   That's not proper food is it?

That's not going to get you through the night is it?

I'll tell you what. Tomorrow night I'll bring you in some proper food eh. And we'll have a proper meal together eh?

Grace   . . . OK.

Phil   OK.

Right . . .

German accent then . . . it's silly.

He resumes reading from 'I put on the puzzled act' up to 'I am leaving this morning', persisting rather awkwardly with the German accent.

As he reads, **Becky** *has come in and is watching the scene.*

She slowly gets closer to them. As **Phil** *notices her in the corner of his eye, he gets less animated until finally trailing off. He stops reading when he sees her now she is standing near him. Silence.*

Silence.

Becky   So do you always read Phil or do you . . . do you ever like watching telly or something?

Phil   Yeah, I watch the telly.

Becky   Yeh? What do you like watching?

Susan   I like watching the nature programmes. David Attenborough.

Beat.

Life on Earth.

Ian *enters. Goes to the coffee area, takes out a large can of energy drink from the fridge and watches them from afar.*

Becky   I like that *Don't Tell the Bride*, have you seen that?

Short silence.

Susan   I have.

Becky   It's boss isn't it?

Susan   Yeah . . .

Becky   Did you see that one last week where he goes skydiving and they say their vows in the air and spanks all the money / it was fucking hilarious cos all she wanted was a big white church wedding.

Phil   Yeah, Richard he had a big white church wedding /

Ian   Yeh, I'm a spiritual person.

Beat.

You know, like Richard says he's religious but his parents are just Catholic that's all that is . . .

Grace   Oh I saw Richard wearing a cross round his neck / so.

Ian   That doesn't mean anything. You don't know what you're talking about.

Silence.

Susan   Are you a religious man then, Ian? /

Ian   No, I'm not religious, Susan, I'm not religious. I'm a spiritual person that's a different thing.

Susan   I think it's /

Ian (*sitting down at the table with them*)   Look I'm going to let you in on something . . . I've thought about this, I've read a lot of books . . . all the . . . great texts.. They all talk about the same shit right. Like I *know* actually what my life is and how the rules of my life are rules for life.

Short silence.

Grace   Have you got a god?

Ian   In some ways, looking at it subjectively . . . I AM my own god.

Beat.

Grace   You should write about that you / might make some money.

Ian   I might well do. I might well do because you know what? It's about really, is really taking the time to you know *be* as strong as you can be – and calling on your own natural, well sexual, energy. Because let's face it this country is full of people that will, anyway that energy is different for men and women – and like I'm . . . (*Searches for words.*) . . . I'm probably more connected to that kind of thing than you are – and that difference causes men and women to not understand like /

Becky (*suddenly coming to the table*)   What you saying, Ian, are you saying you're like better than all of us?

Ian   No I'm not saying that. You've got the wrong end of the stick . . . /

Becky   Yeh?

Ian   Yeh. What I'm trying to say is that . . . Phil? Phil?

Phil *is reading his book.*

Phil? If all men got together and just were like, um . . . we could sort this shit out, right, and that's not sexist or racist, but it wouldn't be a bad thing. I'm not racist, it's not about what colour, Grace, your skin or anything like that.

Susan   What's the message?

Ian   There is no message really, it's not a belief system, it's a way of thinking *critically* right, like I'm focused on what I *can achieve*, in my life yeh, because in my life I've got a lot of experiences. Consciousness of experiences. Like, leadership, I mean it's like if you, Susan, you come across to me and ask me about something well I'm going to be able to give you a presentation of myself and, here's the trick, my product (*Get it,* Grace? *Me/my product – same thing*) that is going to convince you. And that's not because of the whole woman thing / it's just that I'm more focused on what it means to be a man.

Very short silence – **Susan** *looks away.*

Ian   So, Grace, like at college I had all these teachers, and they were trying to teach all this stuff and I'm not being arrogant, I'm a humble person, right, you'd say I'm a humble person /

Grace   Yeh /

Susan *has got up and is walking off.*

Ian   Right, I'm humble. So if I'm being really honest with myself, well I kind of already knew what they were trying to teach me.

Short beat.

There's probably a thing out there for woman doing a similar thing for woman, Susan.

Susan   Yep. I'm just going to the toilet.

She goes into the toilet.

Silence.

Ian   Open mind thinking is what I'd call it.

Silence.

It's really simple, Phil. Phil? Phil?

It's really easy you think about . . . in fact I'll do it for you right now. Just think about what do you want from your life, really think about it. Anything.

He gets out a pen, and takes a leaflet from the table.

What do you want? Phil. Take a moment, what do you want?

Phil   I want more money.

Ian (*writing as he speaks*)   'I want money.'

Phil   And I want to see my daughter.

Ian   Brilliant. 'I want to see my daughter.'

I've written it down for you. (*He rips the leaflet.*) Take it. Memorise it. Meditate on the possibility of it becoming a reality . . . and it'll happen for you.

Short silence.

Phil   Thanks, Ian.

Silence.

Ian   Right, that's lunch.

They all get up.

Ian   Actually I can't give you Saturday off, Becky.

Becky   Ian, Ian!

Ian (*leaving*)   Sorry no.

Becky   Ian please!

Ian   It's not up for discussion.

Grace *and* **Phil** *go out too.* **Becky** *is left alone.*

Becky   Fuck!

She throws her stuff down. She thinks for a moment then takes up her phone, and holds it to her ear. She speaks softly.

She makes a phone call.

Throughout the following scene, the lights get dimmer.

Becky   Hello?

Hiya, sweetheart.

It's your mum . . .

Yes.

Pause.

It's good to hear you.

Listen, sweetheart, I'm really sorry I can't come up this weekend.

Yeh I know I know I said I'd be there but I can't get the time off work. I'll come visit you soon I promise.

Sweetheart?

I'm sorry.

I'm sorry.

/ I would be there if I could . . .

Her daughter hangs up.

Sweetheart?

Sweetheart!

Susan *suddenly comes out of the loo.*

Beat.

Becky   Break's over!

She goes off, fast.

Susan *takes a few steps into the room, and realising she is alone, goes back to the toilet. She comes back with a roll of loo paper.*

She sits at the at the table. Takes out the biscuits she stole from **Grace** *in Break 1 and rolls them up in loo roll. She takes one biscuit and nibbles it rapidly. Puts the rest and the loo roll back into her bag. She peers up at the roof, where one of the fluorescent lights has begun to flicker. She stands to go and join the others and work.*

Blackout.

Act Two

Scene One

Grace *and* **Phil** *eat together. The following night.*

The room is empty – they have skipped their break to be able to finish earlier.

Phil Come in make yourself at home.

Grace Do you want some help?

Phil No no you just sit yourself there.

Beat.

Right, music!

He goes and puts on music on the radio that's the other side of the room. 'Follow Me, Follow You' by Genesis, comes on.

Grace Oh, that's nice.

Phil It's Genesis.

Beat.

This is from when Phil Collins was the lead singer. Before that it was a bloke called Peter Gabriel, and it was rubbish.

It was all about the image, they used to dress up like sunflowers and . . . Phil Collins is different, it's all about the music . . . Anyway, I'm going on a bit!

Beat.

Food!

He goes to get the food he has brought out of the fridge.

Phil So we've got pasta salad, it's got some olives in it, mozzarella . . .

Pause. They eat, the music plays in the background.

Grace How long have you been working here?

Phil About two years.

Grace You seem to get on with Ian.

Phil Yeh we get on really well.

Grace Are you drinking buddies or?

Phil No . . . more workmates . . .

Beat.

But there's a mutual respect.

Grace   Yeh, yeh . . .

Phil   I mean it's not what I planned to do . . .

Short time.

How are you finding things?

Grace   Yeah, I'm good, /

Phil   It's fine /

Grace   It's fine.

Phil   I think we are going to be /

Grace/Phil   Good friends /

Grace   Yeh.

Beat.

Phil   If you don't mind me asking, how old are you?

Grace   Twenty-seven.

How old are you?

Phil   Oh I'm fifty.

Beat.

Phil   It's my daughter's birthday today.

Grace   Ah bless her.

Phil   She's seventeen.

Beat.

I'll tell you what . . . just wait there a minute.

He goes to turn the music off.

Phil   Just hang on.

He runs to the kitchen area where there is a plastic bag. He comes in with the cake that he's taken out of it, there is one candle on it already. He's also lowered the lights.

Grace   Oh wow! Lucky her!

Phil   I was going to have this later . . . but I thought, maybe, we could, you know sing her happy birthday to her and . . .

Grace   Oh . . . /

Phil   And then we could (*he lights the candle.*) blow out the / candles.

Grace   You should probably do it . . . she knows you . . . you're her / dad.

Phil   We could both do it, it'd be a laugh . . . if you don't mind?

Grace   For a laugh . . . yeh, /

Phil   Alright? You don't have to if you / don't want to.

Grace   Yeh, alright, for a laugh alright!

Phil   Alright /

Grace   You could record it, if you've got a phone and if she's got internet then . . .

Phil   Yeh . . . that'll be fun /

Grace   You could send it to her, if she's got email and stuff you . . . (*Getting up and going around the table to sing.*) what's her name?

Phil   Sandra.

Grace   OK . . . Sandra,

Phil   Alright?

Grace   Yeh.

They are both round the table now.

Phil   OK, here we go, ready?

Grace   Yeh.

Phil   Alright, here we go . . .

He crouches down so both the cake and their two faces are in shot.

Phil   Ha!

Grace   Hap!

Phil   OK! Happy . . . come on!

Phil/Grace   Happy birthday to you, happy birthday to you, happy birthday, dear . . .

Phil   Sandra /

Grace   Sandra, happy birthday to you.

Phil (*under his breath*)   Blow out the candles.

They blow out the candles.

To the phone-camera:

Love you, darling!

They stand back up and look at the phone. A time. Silence.

Grace   It didn't record did it . . .

Phil   No.

Silence. He moves away a little.

Grace   We could do it again.

Phil   Oh, maybe, is that OK? Do you mind?

Grace   No, no.

Phil   Is that alright?

He's already going to light the candle.

I'll do it right this time.

Grace   Ha /

Phil   Oh, wait wait . . . OK.

Phil/Grace   Happy birthday to you, happy birthday to you, HAPPY BIRTHDAY, DEAR SAA /

Ian *bursts in from the side door, turns on the lights to full power and charges through the space.*

Ian   Phil that needs to go away now we're having a team meeting thank you.

He goes to the other side and calls to the factory areas.

RIGHT TEAM MEETING PLEASE – TEAM MEETING.

Team Meeting 1

Ian *goes to the centre of the space.* **Phil** *and* **Grace** *put away the food, and slowly gather along with* **Susan** *and* **Becky** *who are coming in still wearing cleaning gloves and tabards, into a semi-circle formation, which is the established team formation for such meetings.*

A short time. Silence. No one looks at **Ian** *in the eye.*

Ian   I'm not happy.

Beat.

What did I ask you to do before the end?

Susan   Clean.

Ian   *Clean.* Clean the room. Are you happy with what you've done?

Grace   Yeh.

Ian   I'm not. Yeh, someone's mopped the floor, someone's scrubbed the toilet . . . But you were specifically asked to finish the wall before you / get a break.

Becky   Ian there's not enough time to get it / it's the end of the shift.

Ian   The work has been assessed for this amount of time so if you go over the allocated (**Becky**'s *phone makes a loud sound, that of a text message being delivered.*) time, turn that off, I'll find someone who can do it more quickly . . .

Becky *starts to read the message – it is a message from List Recruitment saying that they are getting paid late.*

Ian   Get the sprays, get the cloths, get back to the wall. Finish the work, it doesn't matter what time it is.

Becky   Fuck. We're not getting paid till Tuesday now /

Ian   Put that away, take it up with your agency.

Becky   Did you know this /

Susan *has come right up to* **Becky** *and grabbed the phone to read it.*

Ian   It's nothing to do with me. To the wall please.

To the wall.

He exits.

Grace *and* **Phil***, go to the wall,* **Becky** *does too.* **Susan** *stays frozen on the spot. They all have their backs to the audience, three of them up against the wall.*

Becky   Fucking hell I can't even fucking travel.

She exits after **Ian**.

Becky   Ian!

Susan *wanders up to the wall – doesn't really clean.*

Grace   Are you OK, Susan?

Susan   Yes . . .

Are you with List, Grace?

Grace   No, OSS.

Susan   So this doesn't affect you?

Grace   Not that I'm aware of.

Susan   .

Susan *wanders around, she begins to hide her face, which is in tears. She goes to another part of the room, near to where the bleach is. She hides herself. Stands immobile.*

Becky *comes back in rapidly and grabs her spray.*

Susan   Becky does that mean that the actual money is in our account on Tuesday or it's sent on Tuesday but might / be there after that?

Becky   Susan, I don't know.

Susan   .

A time, they clean in silence.

Ian *comes back in.*

Ian   Right sorry, one of the crates has got some spillage in the dry store can you all go and sort it out now, please.

Phil   Don't you want us to finish the wall?

Ian   No go now please.

They all run out.

Ian *sits at the table, vacant. He gets his phone out and flicks through it. He puts on a porn film. The sound is quite loud, he watches it impassively. Switches it off. Sits. Goes to the toilet.*

The warehouse is empty and time passes.

Empty stage. A time.

The lights flicker in the emptiness. After a time, they come back to normal.

Becky *borrows money from* **Grace**.

The cleaners all re-enter, in their coats, finally leaving their shift.

First, **Becky** *and* **Grace**.

Becky   Which way you going?

Grace   Just up the road I'm getting my first bus from there.

Becky   Grace could you lend us twenty quid?

Grace   What?

Becky   Can you lend me twenty quid?

Grace   Oh it's just that I have to repay a loan /

Becky   It's only till Tuesday.

Grace   Right. OK. *Pause.* OK.

I don't actually have any cash though /

Becky   There's a cashpoint down the road.

Grace   OK.

Becky   Right thanks, Grace.

Ian *exits the toilet, goes across the stage.* **Susan** *and* **Phil** *are coming in now, dressed to leave.*

Becky   See you later, Ian.

Grace   Bye.

All exit, **Susan** *hangs back.* **Ian**'s *switched off the lights, so they are now at a very low level.*

Susan (*calling after the others*)   I'm just going to fetch something. See you tomorrow!

She goes back into the space.

She is alone in the space. In the darkness, she looks for a place to sleep.

She lines up three chairs and spreads herself across them.

A time. Silence.

Ian *re-enters finally. He goes towards exit. Sees her.*

He watches her. Goes closer to her.

Ian   You can't sleep here. It's private property.

Susan   No I wasn't sleeping.

Ian   What were you doing?

Susan   I wasn't sleeping. I forgot something and I came back to get it.

Ian   Right you got it?

Susan   Yeh, I got it.

Ian   Good. Well . . .

Susan *still isn't moving.*

Ian   You got somewhere to go then.

He wants to edge her closer to the door.

Susan   Yeh I /

Ian   Good, good. Well . . .

Susan   . . .

. . . Shall I clean that up? /

She's moving towards one of the crates in the corner.

Ian   No. No Susan, Susan, the shift is finished.

OK, alright . . .

Good night.

Good night?

Susan   Yep, good night.

Susan *finally leaves.*

Ian *stands still.*

Blackout.

Scene Two

Team Meeting 2. Another day. 2 am, end of shift.

The lights come up on the assembly again in team-meeting formation.

Ian   I'm happy.

Yeh, I'm happy.

Good night's work . . . well done. Good shift, good team effort.

So the big news is that Richard has let us know they've decided to bring forward the launch of the new sausage by twenty-four hours.

They are going to be called 'Provençal', they've got thyme in them, from Provence.

Phil   That's in France isn't it?

Ian   No idea. What it means is that the machinery all needs to be dismantled and scrubbed out and then they need to re- assemble it to change over the lines. The good news is I do have more hours for everyone. OK?

Beat.

So the way it will work, I'll just cup it onto the end of your shift you've done your 10–2 am. You'll have a couple of hours to kill then 4–9 am cleaning. It's an extra £31.55 in your pockets . . .

Beat.

Now, it does start tonight . . .

Grace   What?

Ian   Me and Phil have done a couple of back to back shifts before haven't we, Phil?

Phil   Yeh.

Ian   You were fine weren't you?

Phil   Yeh but . . . /

Ian   So Phil will probably take the hours . . . if I'm honest I'm sort of expecting everyone to take these hours really. You going to do it for me, Phil?

Phil   Yeh.

Ian Great, yeh, Becky, yeh?

Becky Alright.

Ian Grace?

Grace It's overtime, so it's time and half pay.

Ian It's £31.55.

Beat.

You think about it.

What I will say is that we are looking, well we're thinking about appointing another member of the hygiene team to join Phil and go full time, well thirty hours a week. So obviously this is a good chance to get yourself noticed . . .

Grace *suddenly wanders off upstage to the table, out of the team formation.*

Ian Also I'll also be taking a minute with each of you to do your one on one evaluations and that's just a nice chance for us to talk about how we think you're at how you're prog . . . GRACE can you come back. We are not finished.

Grace *pauses, but then returns slowly to the group.*

Just a nice chance to feedback so we can both see where you're at. So sort of like a pre-interview but nothing serious.

You going to do those hours for me, Grace?

Grace Yeh.

Ian Fantastic.

So it's going to be the tracks, the meat grinding equipment and the lines and it's a machine clean so obviously standards do need to be /

Becky A machine clean? I don't know what that is. /

Susan I haven't had that training.

Ian You don't need any other training. The products are a bit stronger, but it's the same thing, basically . . .

OK so if everyone's happy to proceed, I'll see everyone back here in a couple of hours . . .

They begin to leave.

Sorry, sorry! Just one more minute, just quickly.

Beat – they regroup.

Staff party coming up . . .

Phil. Me and Phil always have a good time at the staff party don't we, Phil?

Phil Yeh.

Ian   It's just a nice chance for the cleaners to mix with the normal staff and . . . It's fancy dress. Phil you had a great costume last year, what was it again?

Phil   Superman.

Ian   You got it from the costume shop . . . /

Phil   No, I made it.

Ian   Good.

Beat.

Well the theme is superheroes.

Phil   Again.

Ian   Yeh.

Becky   Can we all come as you, Ian.

Ian   Hilarious.

So for the party just arrive a bit earlier than you normally would for your shift. They usually bring down some wine, everyone normally brings something to share and we all get a bit drunk and, go crazy.

Beat.

Right. Thank you very much.

They all leave.

Ian   Oh, Grace, can I have a word with you?

Beat.

You're on a verbal warning now for underachieving.

Grace   Is that about . . . is it about last week I said I'm sorry /

Ian   I've accepted your apology /

Grace   Good /

Ian   No not good. You need to keep up with everyone else. OK /

Grace   Well yeh but I did say if you start me off on something small and /

Ian   And I said I can't put you different tasks it's a group effort you need to do the same as everyone else is doing and keep up /

Grace   Yeh but then we can all finish at the same time and I can do the tasks that are easier for me /

Ian   Grace it's nothing personal. Let's take the warning and /

Grace   But I have a condition /

Ian   Grace, let's take the warning and move on.

Take the warning.

Thank you. Grace thank you.

Grace *walks off fast.*

Beat.

Ian   Susan, I'll do your evaluation now, yeh?

Just grab a seat.

Susan *'s evaluation.*

Ian *brings a chair downstage away from the table. Susan does the same. She bumps into the chair.*

Susan   Oh sorry.

Ian   OK I've marked your evaluation sheet up.

So the statements you were asked to reflect on were – just to recap:

I am orderly

I am absorbed with ideas

I am calm

I'm lively

I am argumentative

And I enjoy time pressure.

So we'll just work our way through and see where we agree and disagree and where we match up.

Let's start with the first one – I am orderly. You said you don't know. I gave you a disagree for that because you're not massively good at getting the mops back in the right order and the way you put the products back isn't ideal. Also a couple of times you've mopped the floor before sweeping it so, that's why you've got a disagree.

Not strongly disagree though cause sometimes you do get it right, but there are occasions where you do get it wrong.

Susan   I can do that better.

Ian   Good, under 'I am absorbed with ideas', you said you neither agree or disagree, I gave you strongly disagree for that, I don't know if you agree but I haven't seen any initiative with regards to cleaning or cleaning techniques, or ways to make yourself go a bit faster. I mean would you say you are an ideas person?

Susan   Yes, I would say I'm an ideas person. I've got a lot of ideas /

Ian   What . . .

Susan   What I've written there doesn't mean I'm not absorbed / with ideas.

Ian   OK, alright, what kind of ideas?

Phil *has come in and sits at the table above. Reading his book.*

Susan   I've got lots of ideas about lots of things. About the world. I think I might have misunderstood the question . . .

Ian   I'm just looking for something specific.

Susan   Yep . . . I'm against animal cruelty, and I'm happy to discuss climate change with you. /

Ian   OK, OK / I understand.

Susan   Sorry if I misunderstood /

Ian   No that's fine. It's fine.

Becky *comes in and sits at table too.*

Ian   You've also said 'strongly agree' to 'I am calm' and under 'I am lively' you've said 'disagree'.

Aren't you lively? I've put disagree there too, but I'm willing to, you know take a moment to discuss that 'disagree'.

If that's a disagree you agree to discuss?

Susan   I'm happy to discuss it.

Ian   Just cos I'm looking for someone to join the full-time hygiene team that's you know fun to have around the place, energetic . . . You know someone that's lively to have around the place as well.

Do you think you could be more lively?

Susan   Yes, I could be more lively.

Ian   I'm thinking about all this.

Susan   OK.

Ian   Under argumentative you've put 'disagree' I put disagree there too, so that's good.

Susan   Great.

Beat.

Ian   Under 'I enjoy time pressure' you said 'disagree' so just think about that and question . . . what practical steps do you think you could take to make you enjoy time pressure more?

Susan (*hesitates*)   I don't know . . .

Ian   Right.

Writes a whole lot on his sheet. **Susan** *is worried.*

Susan   I mean /

Ian (*briefly looking up from his papers*)   . . . No, no I think that felt honest. If you don't know that's fine . . .

Susan   OK.

A short time. Silence.

I think I can do a good job.

Ian *ignores this, keeps writing.*

Ian   OK, thanks Susan.

He puts his chair back at the table. Exits.

Can you put your chair back, Susan?

She takes her chair to the table, making a small skip on the way. She sits with the others. Stands up, breathes out. Exits.

Becky   So has he found them horses yet?

Phil   What?

Becky   The bloke in your book?

Phil   No.

A time.

Becky   So when you're not reading or watching *Life on Earth* . . . what do you like to do, Phil?

Phil   I like to cook.

Becky   Are you any good?

Phil   Last night I cooked this pasta dish and it had some broccoli in it / and ham . . .

Becky   I don't like broccoli.

Phil   And.

A time.

Becky   You don't say much do you?

Phil   .

She waits, and then stands up fast, goes to the wall with her phone.

Becky   Why do you always look at me like I'm a cunt?

She puts on Adele's 'Hometown Glory' – drum and bass remix by High Contrast, on her phone. It plays from the speakers of her phone.

Phil   I don't . . .

Becky   What?

Phil   I don't look at you . . . in that way . . .

Becky   I'm sorry is my music disturbing you?

Short time.

She begins to pace around. Somewhere between a boxer getting ready for a fight and a dance.

Phil   If you could just . . .

Becky   Oh do you want to read your book?

What if I want you to put your book down.

The music is building towards the 'drop'.

Fucking hell.

Phil   Becky if you don't mind, could you please turn it down . . .

She kicks something. The music drops, and plays through the theatre's loudspeakers. She continues to talk at him, but we can't hear the words. After a time she stops and goes and stands still. Phil looks at her, softly. She looks at him. He holds her gaze for a moment.

Blackout.

Act Three

Scene One

Machine clean 1. Later that night, into morning.

They have been cleaning machines and moving them through the loading bay back to another area. They are now standing in the space. **Phil** *opens the doors and medium sized machinery comes in. Dismantled meat-grinding equipment that's filthy. They have a limited amount of time to do a colossal job.*

Grace *is moving very slowly now. They are all placing wooden boarding on the floor to protect the equipment. The smell of the products is very strong.*

Susan   Just one?

Phil   Yeh.

Grace *tries to join in.*

Ian   Not you.

The equipment is still coming in.

A quite long time as they just clean it, and the audience watches this.

Ian *goes to the fridge to get a large can of energy drink.*

He gets up and watches, supervises, **Grace** *isn't scrubbing hard enough, her machine is full of nooks and crannies.* **Ian** *stands over her.*

Grace   Am I going fast enough, Ian?

Ian   It's not about going fast enough it's about doing it properly.

You need to start with the rollers.

Grace   I'm starting at the bottom now so . . .

Ian   OK well the dirty water's going to drip off the rollers onto the bottom so / you're wasting your own time

Grace   Well if I finish the bottom bit first /

Ian   Phil?

Phil can I just borrow you for a second, mate?

If she cleans the dirty roller second, is the dirty water going to drip onto the bottom?

Phil   . . . Well it depend/s

Ian   No NOT IT / DEPENDS. YES OR NO.

Grace   But I'm /

Phil   . . . Yes

Ian   Thank you. Clean the rollers.

She does it. He watches and then exits.

She is tired. Stops for a minute.

Phil *comes over to her.*

Phil   Grace I'm sorry /

Grace   Leave me alone, Phil.

Phil   If I can just help /

Grace   LEAVE ME ALONE, Phil.

Phil   .

Ian *comes back in. He has a folder.*

Goes over to **Phil**.

Ian You know you need to scrub harder than that. Exactly.

Goes over towards **Becky** *who is on her hands and knees. Stares at her from behind briefly.*

Ian   Have you scrubbed there underneath /

Becky   Yep.

Ian   You nearly finished that, Sue?

Susan   Yep, yes.

Ian (*pointing to* **Grace**'*s machine on which she is making no progress*)   Do you want to jump on to this one for me?

Grace   No I can do it myself.

Ian *ignores her.* **Susan** *comes rushing around to* **Grace**'*s machine.*

Grace   I don't need her to help me.

A time.

Ian *goes over back behind* **Becky**. *He stares at her. She notices after a time, goes back to her scrubbing harder. Looks at him. Goes back to her scrubbing.*

A short time.

Becky   I'm going for a cigarette.

Ian   Break's not for ten minutes.

Becky *is already walking out.*

Ian   Becky!

BECKY!

A time. **Ian** *finishes his drink in one gulp.*

Ian   Right, Phil, come and get the rest of the products to finish these – you too Susan.

Susan   What?

Ian   The sanitiser sprays.

He and **Phil** *exit.* **Susan** *goes to follow.*

Grace   Susan.

Susan   .

Grace   Susan! Susan . . .

Susan   What, Grace . . . I've got to go and /

Grace   Susan please.

She motions her over. She is in tears.

I can't get up.

My muscles are frozen.

Susan   .

She helps her up slowly.

Come on. Come on.

Do you want a chair?

Grace   Wait just a minute . . . /

Susan   Break's in five minutes, Grace. /

Grace   Susan please.

Susan   Break's in five minutes.

She rushes off back to **Ian** *and* **Phil**, *exits.*

Grace *begins to mutter to herself. It is the Lord's Prayer, but we can't make out the words. She stares out front. Trembling. She's trying to stretch her legs, but they are resisting.*

A time.

Phil *enters, sits. Takes his book to read. Doesn't look at her.*

Grace *stops muttering. Doesn't look at him.*

Struggling for her words:

Grace   I don't know why Ian doesn't . . .

Think I can . . . I don't . . . I can do things in my own way.

He doesn't seem to know that when I'm doing it on my own then that's when we finish on time . . .

He always thinks that. It's better to get everyone to do one thing but if we all . . .

If I start where I'm supposed to start and finish . . . we'll finish . . .

I told him. I say it positively. Because I'm a positive person.

I'm a hard worker. I don't push him to the . . . you know I don't go out for breaks when I'm not supposed to. I don't stay in the loo when I'm not supposed to.

If I was that kind of person I could have him done for discrimination . . . I just get on with things you know.

I could work whatever days he wanted. I could do whatever hours he puts down. The only days I couldn't do were church and that's Sundays but I don't care about that anymore, I've missed it twice.

You know I've missed my meds because I know he gets a bit funny about . . .

Breaks and he doesn't seem to get . . . maybe if I just have a one to one he'll get frustrated . . . and if I could be in the office and . . . he doesn't respect me . . .

She keeps muttering. And then suddenly stops.

Phil How long you been going?

Grace Church?

Phil Yeh.

Beat.

Grace About six months.

Phil Just take a rest hey. Get your head down. Hey?

A time.

Grace *starts to put her plastic gloves back on, and to take the spray thereafter. As if she wants to go to work.*

Phil Grace . . . just have a break.

Just put your head down and . . .

He gets her his jumper and rolls it up to a pillow which he puts on the table.

At a whisper.

Grace, Grace, Grace.

She's about to get up so he begins to read from his book, from 'The horse put his feet' to 'and where he could go, I went to'.

As he does, she begins to lie down and throughout the following falls asleep.

Becky *has come in unnoticed.*

Phil *lays his jacket over* **Grace**'s *shoulders. Moves towards the door. On his way notices* **Becky**. *Freezes.*

Phil   She's asleep.

He moves forward. **Becky** *blocks his way, so that he is cornered by the roll cages. He steps forward and she blocks him with her head on his chest.*

A short time.

Phil   Becky . . . stop, Becky.

Becky *moves up and kisses him – he stretches his hands above her to not touch her but finally does respond.*

She takes off his belt and pulls down his trousers. Pushes him into a corner, undresses. Pushes him to the ground and they have sex.

It lasts for a short time. **Phil** *begins to cry during the act.* **Becky** *moves away fast after.* **Phil** *holds her for as long as he can, from the floor. She puts her clothes on.*

A time . . . **Phil** *is rolled in a ball on the floor. Silence.*

Phil (*softly*)   I'm sorry.

I'm sorry.

He gets dressed.

Goes towards **Becky** *who is a couple of metres away at least.*

I'm sorry . . .

Becky *gestures for him not to.*

It's OK.

No.

He moves away, towards the table. He goes to his book.

He sits down. They both stay immobile. Silence. A time.

Susan *enters. She sits at the table.*

A short time.

Susan   Has he found his horses yet?

Phil   .

A short time.

Ian *enters. Goes to the double doors. From this point on, a large bass sound is pulsing . . . It has been used throughout the piece but comes to the fore now.*

Ian   Phil.

Ian *and* **Phil** *bring in huge machines this time, on rollers, they are the machinery, it fills the stage. They all silently get up and clean. This time it is so dirty that they need buckets of hot water or hoses to clean down the objects.*

The lights begin to dim. The pulse is very loud and very bass heavy. Over several minutes, they clean, until the noise is deafening, and the light flickers. **Grace** *looks out at one moment and then back to her cleaning. It suddenly blacks out.*

End.

Acknowledgements for *Beyond Caring*

Thanks to the following: Mélanie Lomoff, Finbar Mostyn-Williams, Felicity Hilton, Jay Miller and all the team at The Yard, Colin Jenkins, Jessica Rose Boyd who performed in an earlier workshop draft, Charlotte Holness and all at St Mungo's Broadway, Lucila Granada at LAWA, Catherine Whittaker and all at UNITE, Adrian Gregory at Extraman Recruitment, the Equality and Human Rights Commission, Ruth Barnett, Margaret Zeldin, Peter Brook and Marie-Helène Estienne, Iwona Rybak and all the cleaning staff at the National Theatre, Ben Power and all the team at the NT, Giles Smart and Anna Brewer.

Special thanks to Sonia and Erica, without whom this play would not have been possible.

Introduction to *LOVE*: Have a Heart
Daniel Loayza

Not much happens in *LOVE*. Nothing, in any case, that normally happens in a play: suspense, reversals of alliances, certainties that collapse, startling revelations and so on. There is perhaps only one such element in the play. All the more reason not to reveal it in an introduction. Suffice to say that we get acquainted with people who are waiting for something (maybe that is saying too much already). Are they right to do so? Will their expectations be met? Reading these lines, you might anticipate a commentary of some new version of *Waiting for Godot.* I'd better stop right away.

LOVE is divided into three acts, subdivided (with one exception) into scenes. In Act I, there are two moments from the same day in winter (morning and afternoon); in Act II, the beginning of another week, then we move on to about five hours later; a single scene makes up the whole of Act III. These few scenes are set in a single location and constructed like Chekhovian acts. Their development is uninterrupted. While they run their course, the stage is left empty (or almost so) more frequently than in Chekhov, due to the comings and goings of the actors. This comes as no surprise, given Zeldin's avoidance of the curtain.

Within this Chekhovian rhythmic framework, Zeldin composes his own 'music' (he often refers to his work as 'music'). The list of characters in *LOVE* provides us with at most three kinds of descriptive information: age, professional status, family situation. Each of the characters represents an original combination of these variables. None is satisfactory, if only because no one is in paid employment, although many of them are seeking it. What is left of humanity when a human being no longer has a 'productive' existence? What are the consequences of the official, administrative confusion between the economic and the social – between livelihood and life?

In this key, the melodies of this 'music' are the lifelines followed by each individual character. We meet Paige, who is trying to rehearse her song in a Nativity play, and her older brother Jason, a teenager who tends to withdraw into his headphones. At the opposite ends of the age spectrum, there is an unborn child and a very old and sick woman, Barbara, whose final exit from the stage takes on a meaning that is not lost on any member of the audience. Between these extremes, both situated beyond the realm of 'responsibility', the other characters pursue various 'adult' objectives: find a job, obtain housing, assert rights, fight bureaucracy. All of this is more often than not improvised under the pressure of circumstances and takes place on a day-to-day basis under one and the same roof, inside the temporary accommodation that has been given to them by the Council.

When melodies resonate in the same room, either they follow one another in a sufficiently distinct manner to avoid cacophony, or they overlap. When they do, there is no reason why they should produce harmonious chords. If certain general guidelines guarantee some sort of overall order, so much the better: a lunch or a dinner can take place without too many clashes. But the order in which people go to the toilet – especially when there is only one – causes tension that cannot always be resolved by negotiation. The same applies to obtaining social housing, as each person considers his or her own emergency to take precedence. To attend a performance of *LOVE* is to experience 'music' made up of almost consonant chords, shot through with strident flares whenever resources of any kind (time, space, priority, privacy) are found lacking. It is to feel the pulsations of the latent violence such conditions of existence entail, but also the endlessly renewed effort to fight back and build, despite the hardships, a common space that might be truly shared. It is to witness the confrontations that can lead from repulsive proximity (a woman's dressing gown soiled by another woman's faeces) to overwhelming intimacy (the light touch of a man's hand on a pregnant woman's belly).

Promiscuity, excessive proximity, leads to shouting. Intimacy is conducive to silence. Between one and the other, Zeldin's characters grope for some sort of balance. This is not easy, as the characters in *LOVE* are anything but eloquent. In Chekhov's dramas, sociological diversity allows for a certain variety in the verbal palette: his theatre has no shortage of more or less authentic intellectuals, students, doctors, who are capable of delivering theoretically charged tirades. Zeldin's characters have no such command of language. Their syntax is tentative, their utterances few and often broken (sometimes reduced to a single dot, which in Zeldin's personal symbolic notation indicates 'a thought that does not become a word').

Zeldin's 'music' is not solely or mainly verbal. Every literary text carries different sorts of layers, intimate or social, real or fantastical, historical or contemporary; different geographies too. Theatrical texts are no exception. In order to lay bare their specific quality, let us remove all of these layers, one by one. The more the textual aspect fades out, the better we perceive the utterly theatrical constituents: place, body and witness – the three defining points of the theatrical triangle within which Alexander Zeldin operates, for he is acutely aware of the non-textual character of his trade. With his own tools and in his own way, he seems to be conducting a theatrical investigation that reflects on Beckett's lessons. Like Beckett, by dint of reducing the verbal part of theatre, Zeldin achieves forms whose sheer simplicity intensifies the experience of theatrical presence. Beckett's search, however, is silence-bound, beyond all history and society; the presence he achieves is that of mortal bodies haunted by their destruction, in an empty place that remains to be inhabited, whereas the presence that captivates Zeldin is firmly rooted in history and society. It is not so much, or not only, mortality that inspires his current work: rather, it is poverty as a concrete, social fact. In Beckett's drama, the body can be reduced to a nameless, almost generalized figure. For Zeldin, in contrast, poverty is not just a sociological costume or economic determination which would have to be removed in order to let us reach the deeper, underlying level – that of mortality, understood to be more general, more metaphysically worthy of *Dasein*[1]. Nor does poverty according to Zeldin lend itself to be interpreted as a (more or less humanistic) metaphor for anything else. Rather, what Zeldin shows is that the ontological reality of poverty should not be dismissed too quickly. But mortality, although fundamental, all too often distracts us from it, if only by fascinating us, acting as a screen or a mask that is all the more formidable since our culture, beginning with Homer, has aestheticized death. Death feeds an infinite number of stories. Perhaps because there is no such thing as a 'never-ending story', and death provides a most convenient ending point: it may be arbitrary, of course, even absurd, but clearer than any other, and always at hand. Poverty, on the other hand, seems to be more of a state than an event: it does not *punctuate* any story.

Yet Zeldin wants to tell stories. But his are of the kind that are difficult to tell. For his theatre, to borrow a phrase from Deleuze, grows from the middle. Therein lies, perhaps, the deepest reason why it is so difficult to introduce such a play as *LOVE:* in some respects, it neither begins nor ends but captures states, producing them, *sounding* them. This is not without risk, as this kind of theatre might seem to come very close to didactic, political theatre, or lead to compassionate melodrama. Some spectators could resist the appeal of *LOVE,* either because they feel the play is an implicit accusation and their emotions are being force-fed, or on the contrary because they believe such a theatrical proposition, and above all their agreeing to witness it, can never replace actual social commitment. In short, Zeldin would awaken the bad conscience of the bourgeois audience only in order to appease it. Though I understand these reactions, I believe Zeldin's theatrical research shows no sign of such emotional or political complacency. His theatre does not raise an explicit challenge, does not point an accusing finger. He merely states and that is enough to denounce, making it all the more terrible and disturbing, as he leads us to *realise* the *reality* of it all.

The pattern of time, the arrangement of actions in *LOVE* are not meant to serve as a filtering stylization of a social reality. There is indeed a form – everything is written, worked on at length, rehearsed, repeatable (which is why *LOVE* deserves to be published in book form). But it is not meant to extenuate or exaggerate what it gives form to (no euphemism here, no melodramatic hyperbole). More subtly, it aims at redirecting our gaze, and then supporting it; at turning it towards objects that it would tend to avoid if left to itself, then keeping it fixed on them. The theatre that interests Zeldin is therefore low key and obscene – a combination that might appear to be contradictory, but which he makes coherent.

Let us return to the three points of the theatrical triangle (place, body and witness). As for space, Zeldin prefers rigorous, almost *trompe-l'oeil* realism: so the critics say, and all the spectators confirm it. But how do they know this, and how do we? As for the bodies, there is nothing distinctly thespian about their ways of being on stage. In the production of *LOVE,* the style of acting showed no trace of what is called 'acting'. The programmes and reviews always specify, moreover, that while some of these bodies are those of professionals, others are those of non-professionals. Why is that? Besides, if artifice only aims to erase itself, in what way would this kind of theatre differ from certain hyper-realistic productions? This, I believe, is where the third, sharpest vertex of the triangle comes in. Zeldin's work is not a *trompe-l'oeil* because it does *not* mean to 'deceive' the 'eye'. Not that Zeldin has forgotten the lessons of Brecht, but he belongs to a generation that is well aware that even the *V-Effekt,* the laying bare of artistic processes, the dialectical contradiction between naturalness and artificiality, provocation, 'in-yer-face' violence, tend to become tricks of a trade, all too easily assimilated by artists and audiences alike, socially digested to the point where they are ultimately treated as labels, shibboleths, marks of belonging to one club or another (that of enlightened, progressive spectators, etc.). Not only has Zeldin not forgotten that this is (only) theatre – he doesn't try to make us forget it either, nor to remind us of it. As playwright and as director, he trusts his audience. The challenge he presents is of a different sort.

Art can be work and leisure at the same time. Theatre is not necessarily a distraction for the eye; it can offer a means of concentrating it. Such was the case with Greek tragedy, which invited its spectators to take a long look at the unbearable, the unthinkable, the horror: a son who has married his mother; a mad warrior, covered in blood, who commits suicide; a suffering, stinking body, which screams in agony without being able to die. But with the passage of time, even Oedipus, Ajax, Herakles or Philoctetes end up becoming aesthetic, almost decorative objects – chosen tokens of cultural wealth. And our gaze, seduced by a paradoxical pleasure, no longer turns away from them, because it no longer has anything to fear. But poverty is quite another matter. Even tramps, when of the metaphysical kind, make excellent clowns, as Beckett demonstrated – but who spends time with the real ones? Some people, sometimes, throw them a coin, but nobody lingers (the coin is a hasty toll, the price to pay in order to keep walking). Now the tramps, at least, are to be met in the street. But what about the 'ordinary' poor? The threshold under which they fall is not only economic: it shuts them out of our consciousness and perception. Such is the obscenity of poverty – exposed in its full nakedness, is it not ugliness itself, one of the limbs that the social body most urgently tries to cover up? Taking this question seriously, Zeldin has constructed an astonishingly powerful theatrical response to it, as simply and serenely transgressive as Columbus' egg, reminding us that if we are to know what this 'ugliness' is, we must first take a hard, long look at it. His writing is therefore of the kind that rests on long, fixed shots, while his dramaturgy is based on a 'low intensity' intensity, so to speak, with minimal montage of a few moments that seem almost empty, punctuated by sudden (though not unpredictable) crises, taken from fairly long durations (in *LOVE,* a few weeks; in *Faith, Hope and Charity,* a few seasons) and organised so as to let us perceive how banal, everyday time is being relentlessly besieged, undermined, battered, worn out, shattered by medium, or long-term, insecurity (when a bureaucrat gives you forty minutes, without previous notice, to show up at some desk, you can no longer take your daughter to school; when you are forced to look after your old mother without respite, it is as if your future is being devoured by your past).

The only way to make all this felt is to accompany the movements of these bodies in their *real* durations. To treat them, and their ordeals, as objects to be observed behind the isolating glass of a fourth wall would already be to keep them at a distance: the gaze would not turn away from them, but wouldn't consider their humanity. On the other hand, seeking to reduce that distance by taking the audience hostage of their suffering would only lead to an aggravation of the gaps and misunderstandings: the spectators' gaze, aggressively summoned to contemplate what they perhaps did not want to see, would immediately turn away. Zeldin therefore arranges the relationship between stage and audience in such a way that this gaze is given time to accommodate itself and so does not shy away. He likes to recall the Greek etymology of the word *theatron,* 'place where one sees'; in his opinion, this theatrical 'seeing' is more a matter of contemplating than merely glimpsing or looking

Contemplation is not an attitude that can be switched on; it requires time. We must allow our gaze to open up to meditation, reflection or reverie – and to do so freely, without having to come up with articulate answers to predetermined questions, nor having to let such answers be forced upon us, whether they be intellectual or emotional, theses or affects such as terror or pity. According to Zeldin, this free conversion of one's gaze to a contemplative relationship can only take place against the backdrop of an anti-modern, anti-televisual, leisurely tempo, devoid of all frenzy. Accordingly, Zeldin's dramatic 'music' contains many silent pauses. These 'empty' moments, which are an integral part of the action, endow its gestures, its utterances and its forms of presence with a special fullness. Meals, for example, last for the duration of a meal. This reality of duration confirms the impression conveyed by the realistic quality of the set: as a consequence, what is played out in *LOVE* is tacitly considered by the audience to be indistinguishable from reality. Therefore, what we experience is something more than the pleasure of recognition which Aristotle mentions in his *Poetics* ('yes, being poor is indeed just that, it is to live in this kind of place and meet this kind of people, it is to behave in this way and suffer this kind of injustice'). For we now recognise that we recognise – we *realise* ('yes, I knew that being poor is just that, but now I also see that I was avoiding thinking about it or spelling it out for myself'). We recognise that we had already been sharing some sort of unconscious social knowledge (always in need of being explicitly re-stated) of what the play puts before our eyes. The experience is no longer only aesthetic, but ethical.

Alexander Zeldin's theatre, under its simple guise, may turn out to be a difficult reading experience. *LOVE* is not a verbally dazzling play with a dizzyingly complex plot. It needs to be deciphered beyond its words, as it calls for readers eager to consider the actual, lived reality of the experiences noted by the textual score. Its production, far from purporting to make us discover these experiences as a documentary would, invites us to recollect them 'in real time' – precisely the time no book can ever provide. It must therefore be allowed for, 'realised', by the readers themselves as best they can. Such reading requires more than ordinary patience or imagination. One must accept to approach this kind of theatre humbly and without irony, in a spirit of sensitive, generous goodwill that makes encounters between human beings possible. To put it bluntly, you've got to have a heart. After all, the heart is a vital organ that also needs its fair share of training, even if such an exercise may sometimes turn out to be painful or cause discomfort. If you are afraid of suffering this kind of pain – or if you are not afraid at all – expose yourself to the experience, see *LOVE*, at least read it. And if you are not afraid to feel, Zeldin is just the artist for you.

Paris, July 20, 2021

Note

1   German word meaning 'presence'. It is the fundamental concept in the existential philosophy of Martin Heidegger.

LOVE

LOVE received its world premiere in the Dorfman Theatre at the National Theatre, London on 13 December 2016 and opened in The STUDIO at Birmingham Repertory Theatre on 26 January 2017, with the following cast and creative team:

Paige	Emily Beacock
	Darcey Brown
	Grace Doherty
Barbara	Anna Calder-Marshall
Dean	Luke Clarke
Emma	Janet Etuk
Adnan	Ammar Haj Ahmad
Colin	Nick Holder
Jason	Vitaly Outkine
	Yonatan Pelé Roodner
	Bobby Stallwood
Tharwa	Hind Swareldahab

Director	Alexander Zeldin
Set and Costume Designer	Natasha Jenkins
Lighting Designer	Marc Williams
Sound Designer	Josh Anio Grigg
Movement Director	Marcin Rudy
Fight Director	Kev McCurdy
Company Voice Work	Cathleen McCarron
Staff Director	Diyan Zora

LOVE received its European premiere at Odéon Théâtre de l'Europe's Ateliers Berthier on 5 November 2018 with the following cast and creative team:

Adnan	Waj Ali
Paige	Emily Beacock
	Rosanna Beacock
Barbara	Anna Calder-Marshall
Dean	Luke Clarke
Emma	Janet Etuk
Colin	Nick Holder
Tharwa	Mimi Malaz Bashir
Jason	Yonatan Pelé Roodner

Director	Alexander Zeldin
Set and Costume Designer	Natasha Jenkins
Lighting Designer	Marc Williams
Sound Designer	Josh Anio Grigg
Movement Director	Marcin Rudy
Associate Director	Diyan Zora

Characters

Dean, *thirty-one, a father, looking for work*
Emma, *twenty-seven, his partner, studying to be a massage and wellness therapist, stepmother to the children and pregnant*
Paige, *eight, his daughter*
Jason, *twelve, his son*
Colin, *fifty, a man who is a carer to his mother.*
Barbara, *his mother*
Tharwa, *fortyish, a mother without her children*
Adnan, *thirty-fiveish, a man who is injured*

Notes

/ is an interruption

'.' is a thought that doesn't become a word

Act One

Scene One

6.30 am.

Lights come up on the common room of a temporary housing facility. There is a kitchen area with dishes piled up, some tables and chairs. At the top end of the room there are a couple of doorways, through which, when opened, we can glimpse two very cramped bedrooms.

Downstage, there is a toilet, the door of which has been left open and the light on. The room itself is quite dark; it has a feeling of being inhospitable, cold. The only thing sifting through is an overcast December light from the skylight in the roof. There is a tree above the roof that intermittently brushes against the skylight.

The audience are sat around in such a way that the actors can move freely amongst them.

After a time, a woman comes through, **Tharwa**. *She goes to the kitchen with a plastic bag full of food. She makes some toast and puts the kettle on to boil.*

A short time as she waits. She is half turned towards us.

A door upstage opens. **Colin** *comes out in his pants. He hesitates, but crosses the stage to the toilet.*

Tharwa *decides to go back to her room.*

During the above there have been faint noises from the other room: the sound of an alarm clock, children's voices rising above the sound of adults. **Dean** *has woken up* **Jason** *and asked him to get dressed.*

The door of the other room opens. **Dean** *goes to the toilet, with* **Paige**.

Dean   Wait, love.

Paige   I need the loo, Dad, I need the loo.

Dean   Wait, wait, I just need to clean it first.

Paige   Dad.

Dean   Wait there.

As he turns to go back to the toilet **Colin** *and* **Barbara** *are setting out.*

He sends **Barbara** *across to the loo; she gets going before* **Paige** *can.*

Colin   You OK?

Barbara   Yeh . . .

Dean   You go first.

Colin   Cheers, thank you.

Paige *waits silently by the wall, then her father brings her closer to the loo.*

Paige   I want the loo I want the loo.

Dean   OK.

Barbara *leaves the bathroom at last. And shares a look with* **Paige**.

Paige *looks down on the floor.* **Barbara** *goes back to the room.*

Barbara   .

Paige   .

Paige *wants to go in, but* **Dean** *needs to go in first to clean it up.*

Emma *emerges as* **Dean** *is cleaning the toilet and starts removing bottles from the table.*

Dean   You having a wee?

Paige *goes into the bathroom. In the bedroom* **Jason** *turns the iPad on.*

Emma   Dean, can we eat out here?

Dean   Yeh, I'll give it a quick wipe.

As **Paige** *emerges:*

Dean   Have you flushed it?

Right, do it then!

Paige *goes back in and flushes the toilet.*

Dean   Right wash your hands.

Paige *does and then goes to other side of the room.* **Emma** *cleans as* **Dean** *puts plates out.*

Music seeps in from the bedroom.

Emma   Jase, turn it off please.

Dean   Paige, come and sit down please.

He goes to **Jason** *in the bedroom.*

Dean   Turn it down or turn it off mate yeah.

Emma *takes a slice of toast to* **Paige**.

Emma   There you go.

Paige   No I want butter.

Emma   We don't have any but your dad's going shopping later.

Paige   It's disgusting.

Emma   It's just jam, Paige.

Paige   We always have butter. (*She coughs.*)

Emma   Just eat it please. Eat.

Dean *gets butter from another guest's fridge shelf and puts it on* **Paige**'s *toast.*

Emma   What's that?

Paige   I've got a cold.

Dean   No you don't.

Emma   Dean?

Dean   It's fine.

He goes into the room to give **Jason** *toast. He sits next to* **Jason** *on the bed.*

Paige   I want to go to Sarah's party.

Emma   Where is it?

Paige   Airhop.

Emma   What's that?

Paige   It's like trampolining but better.

Emma   OK, well, ask your dad.

The tree brushes the roof. **Paige** *sits staring at the roof.*

Paige   What's that noise?

Emma   It's just the tree.

Jason *crosses the stage with his toothbrush in his mouth.*

Emma   Hey, Jase, you brushing your teeth?

Jason *shows her the toothbrush as if to say 'obviously'.*

He goes into the bathroom. **Dean** *enters.*

Paige   Dad, can I go to Sarah's party?

Dean   What did Emma say?

Paige   She said to ask you.

Dean   I'll think about it.

D'you remember I'm taking them early today.

Emma   Fine.

Dean   I'll sort it out, don't worry.

Jason *exits the bathroom.*

Jason   The sink's fucked.

Dean   Sink's broken.

Jason   Sink's broken and it's fucked.

He goes to spit at the sink, very briefly.

This place is crap, Dad.

Dean   Just think, it's better than your nan's.

Jason   Yeah.

Dean   Yeah well we won't be here long, mate.

Colin *has come in. He looks into the bedroom, the family look at him.*

Paige   I want cereal.

Dean   There isn't any, sorry.

Colin   Breakfast.

Dean   Yeh. We'll be out of your way in a minute.

Colin   Nah nah. You're alright, mate.

A short pause.

I might skip breakfast myself.

Had a bit of a sniffy belly recently.

Paige   I want cereal.

Colin   You alright, mate, haven't met you yet.

Paige   I'm Paige.

Colin   I'm Colin, I live next door. (*He goes to shake her hand; she shakes it.*)

Pause.

I had a takeaway last night, I think that did it.

Chinese, yeh fucking guts are a mess, man.

Emma   Sorry are those yours?

Colin   Yeh. Oh sorry yeh.

I'll just put them in the bin, it's fine.

He clears away a couple of beer cans that were on the table.

A time. The family eat.

Colin   You getting anywhere then?

Dean   Sorry?

Colin   Council.

Dean   Yeh, we're just waiting on them-on a couple of things /

Colin   Twats aren't they?

Dean   I'm going to sort it out today actually.

Paige   I don't want it then.

Dean   Fine, don't eat it then.

Colin   Yeh I'm actually going to see them next week myself I've you know complained and.

.

You working then yeh /

Dean   Yeh.

Well I'm trying to find work but it's difficult isn't it.

Colin   I'm / sorry . . .? I wasn't working I couldn't, health issues but. Yeh I'm developing opportunities at the moment / actually.

D'you mind if I have this? (*He takes a bit of toast.*)

Dean   No, it's fine.

Colin   This is all I can fucking handle.

Barbara *enters.*

Paige   I want Coco Pops.

Dean   I'm going to pick some stuff up later.

Jason   Get some jammy dodgers.

Colin   You alright?

Barbara   Yeah.

Nice egg, settle your tum?

One egg or two?

Colin   Just one yeah.

Emma   Is Sarah your best friend?

Paige   No, I just want to go to her party.

Dean   Where is it?

Paige   Near Sarah's.

Dean   Ooh, that's a long way.

Colin (*to* **Barbara**)   You alright?

Barbara   Yeh.

Emma   Dean shall we . . .

Dean   No.

Colin (*When he touches plate.*)   Fucking wet.

Barbara *goes to pick up a fork at the sink. She feels unwell and stumbles.*

Colin   Oh come on.

Colin *steadies her.*

You alright Mum? I've got you.

Come and sit down, there you go Mum,

Bit too much for you bab, come on lovely.

They cross back to table and sit her down.

Dean   Right come on, let's get ready.

Dean *and* **Paige** *go into the bedroom.* **Colin** *goes back to the kitchen to try and finish cooking the breakfast.*

Barbara   Sorry, Col.

Colin   No, you're alright.

Emma *goes to the kitchen and washes up.*

Emma   Sorry. Sorry. Won't be long.

Colin   No worries.

Emma *goes towards the bedroom as* **Jason** *crosses to the bathroom.*

Colin   They're not yours then the euh . . .?

Emma   No.

She goes into the bedroom.

The branch strokes the roof; the sound is a little like the sound of the sea.

Thinking about the sea, mumbled. **Emma** *goes into the bedroom.*

Barbara (*thinking about the sea, mumbled*)   That sounds a bit like a wave.

Eggy weggy done?

Colin   Eh? Oh for fuck's sake.

It's a bit burnt but I like the dry bits on the bottom you know. It's really nice when you mix them in.

Barbara   Got coleslaw?

Dean *enters with* **Paige**.

Colin   No I'm alright.

Emma *enters.*

Dean   See you later, little man. (*He kisses her stomach.*)

It'll be fine yeah?

Emma   Yeah.

Dean, stay calm.

Dean *kisses* **Emma**.

Dean   Yeah, I'll call you after. It'll be fine.

(*to* **Paige**)   Right, come on you.

Jason! Jason.

Jason *runs out of the bathroom.* **Dean**, **Paige** *and* **Jason** *exit.*

Emma *crosses to the bathroom.*

Colin   No fucking knives.

Colin *uses a spatula to put butter on bread then spends a short time noisily emptying the pan of egg on to the bread.*

Barbara   The sooner you get us out of here the better.

He brings breakfast over.

You did talk to them, didn't you?

Colin   Mum, I'm trying to have my fucking breakfast here yeh. I went two days ago, I'm going Monday, I'll even call 'em if you want but you mithering me isn't helping anyone yeh?

Barbara (*with pity*)   When you was a baby you was very quiet Col.

Colin   Sorry mum.

She goes back into the room.

Pause while **Colin** *eats. He puts his plate by the sink checking that no-one noticed him do it and watches the bathroom as* **Emma** *showers.*

Emma *exits wearing a bathrobe and nothing else. –* **Colin** *stops her on the way.*

Colin   You alright?

Emma   Yep.

Colin   He's off to see them then?

Emma   Yeh / council offices, yeh.

Colin   Yeh? / No.

Emma   No, we're obviously not counting on being here longer / than a few.

Colin   Yeh. Fucking arseholes / aren't they.

Emma   You / sorry.

Colin   Yeh yeh.

Obviously our situations are different but.

Emma   Yeh no of course.

Colin   .

That'll help is all I'm saying.

Stares at her belly.

You got long to go?

Enter **Barbara**.

Emma   I'm thirty-three weeks /

Colin   Nice.

Beat.

Yeh just me and me mum you know.

Emma   Right.

Colin   She'd give me the top brick of the chimney / you've only got your own.

Barbara   He's my carer.

She gives a chocolate bar to **Colin**.

Colin (*quite slow and softly spoken almost as if it were a confession*)   I'm her carer. Just so you know like, when we agreed to move out of our house we went to look at a home right /

Barbara   But there was a woman tied to a chair /

Colin   They just left them there on the floor in piss and shit.

Barbara   And Floyd Mattison.

Colin   Twat, that was our person before we're just.

Barbara   He said we'd get our own flat cos we agreed to move out.

Colin   They just cheat you like we're waiting, fuck, we need somewhere adapted you know our place is like posh flats now /

Emma   Yeh no obviously I don't want – the baby – to be born here /

Colin   No, like obviously yeh but you know they just cheat you.

Emma   Yeah, we were evicted, they put the rent up like overnight and we couldn't afford it /

Colin   You're fucking joking, landlords, vermin, like I'm her carer and you know the council just /don't support you like.

Barbara   What's her name?

The little girl.

Emma   Paige.

Colin   Ah.

Barbara   She's a nice little girl.

She begins to walk towards the toilet – embarrassed.

Excuse me.

When she gets to the toilet there is a pause, she goes in and then looks out from the loo to **Colin***. He goes over to the loo.* **Emma** *runs into the room.*

Colin   D'you need anything?

Barbara   No.

Colin *is aware that* **Emma** *has gone in. He goes back to his bedroom.*

Tharwa *enters; she is alone on stage. She makes a call to her husband and children, speaking in Arabic.*

Tharwa   Ibrahim? Ibrahim? Are you OK? Hello? Give me Tala.

Tala! Tala! Mummy loves you. Tala 'tinkish tinkish'.

She makes the gesture of a star with her hands.

Eventually the signal cuts out.

Adnan *arrives. He is carrying a big rucksack and a separate bag. He tentatively, slowly, enters, coming through the audience.*

Adnan   Excuse me? Do you know where room 8 is?

Tharwa   You go through that door there.

Adnan   Thank you.

He goes to drink water. He wanders upstage.

Here?

Tharwa   Yes.

Here.

Barbara *enters from the bathroom, notices* **Adnan***. He exits through double doors.*

Tharwa *and* **Barbara** *look at each other.*

Tharwa   Good morning, madam.

Silence. They stand still watching each other.

Blackout.

Scene Two

Later that day, 3 pm or so.

Barbara *sitting alone on stage.* **Dean** *enters.*

Simultaneously in the bedroom **Paige** *practises 'Away in a Manger'.*

Dean   Fucking hell.

Paige (*singing*)   Away in a manger.

Barbara   What?

Jason   Shut up, Paige.

Dean   Nothing. Sorry.

Enter **Emma**.

Emma   Dean. Did you see the council? You didn't call.

Dean (*in movement*)   Yeah. I'm just popping to the toilet.

He retreats into the toilet.

Enter **Paige**.

Paige   Dad? Dad, watch me, Dad.

Emma   He'll be out in a minute.

Paige *puts music track on her phone.*

She rehearses 'Away in a Manger'.

Emma *goes over to* **Paige**.

Emma   Uh . . . not here, babe, do it in the room.

Paige   I can't, Jason's being an idiot and there's no space. I need to practise, I have the nativity.

Emma   Yeah well it's too loud.

Paige   Leave me alone.

Can you just go. Please.

Emma   Well just be quiet then.

After a few moments **Paige** *starts singing along to the track.*

Jason (*from bedroom*)   Shut up, Paige, you can't sing.

Emma   Not in here.

(*To* **Barbara**.)   Sorry.

Barbara   It's alright I don't mind.

Emma   .

Sorry. She's practising for this Christmas show.

Moment of slight connection with **Barbara** *for* **Emma**.

Emma *goes into the bedroom.* **Paige** *continues miming the actions to the song.*

Barbara   What you doing then?

Paige   Stars.

Barbara   I was in a nativity once.

Paige *runs off.*

Barbara   I was a shepherd.

Her feelings are hurt. She goes to her room.

Colin. Colin.

They've been to the council.

Emma *is alone onstage.* **Dean** *out of the loo, checking that the coast is clear. We sense that this is already a ritual – to check there is a short moment when there is no one in the space to have dinner.*

Enter **Paige** *from the bedroom. She runs to* **Dean**.

Paige   Dad, Dad, Dad! Jason's being a big bully.

Dean   Is he? Your singing sounded lovely.

He goes to the kitchen. **Paige** *clings to him.*

Paige   Dad, listen to me. (*Singing.*) Away in a manger.

Emma   Dean . . .

Dean   I heard you, it's very good.

Paige   Dad, listen, I want to show you my song.

Emma   Dean . . .?

Dean   Paige, in a minute.

Emma   Paige. I need to talk to your dad.

Paige *runs off.*

Emma   How'd it go?

Dean   It's fine, there's been some sort of mix-up, they've given me a number to call on Monday.

Emma   What kind of mix-up?

Dean   There's been crosswires – remember that appointment we missed at the job centre?

Emma   Yeh, on eviction day? But.

Dean   I swear it's fine, I was there for eight hours, babe, I'm on it.

Kisses her.

(*Picking up the plates.*)   I'll put these out.

Jason *enters with a football.* **Dean** *puts three plates on the table.*

Emma   Dean . . .

Jason   Dad.

He throws the ball to **Dean**.

Dean   What have I told you about playing with that inside?

Plays football with the boy. He then goes and has a pillow fight with him in the room.

Jason   Bullshit.

The food is disappointing.

Dean   Come and sit down. Paige, come on. Turn that off please.

Emma   Your dad's had a bit of a stressful day, didn't get to the shops, so let's not make a fuss and just eat it yeah?

She sits at the table. **Dean** *brings the rice and serves it onto three plates.*

Dean   Hood off at the table, Jason.

Jason   Is that it?

Dean   Hood off at the table.

He sits at the table.

Paige   Where's your dinner, Dad?

Dean   I've already eaten.

Jason   It's not even dinner.

Enter **Adnan**. *He looks into the common room and sees it is busy.*

Paige   Who's that?

Emma   He lives upstairs.

Adnan *exits.*

Dean   How was your day?

Emma   Good. I managed to get an appointment on Monday at the hospital. I think I should just check in.

Dean   Great – Jason?

Jason *shrugs his shoulders.*

Dean   Oh that good eh?

(*To* **Paige**.)   How about you?

Paige   Good. I got a certificate for being kind.

Jason *laughs*.

Dean   Oi!

Paige   I got a certificate / for being kind.

Jason *laughs in her face*.

Dean   Jason! Go on, who gave you that?

Paige   Mrs Watts.

Jason   Shut up.

Paige   Dad's asking me, Jason /

Jason   I don't care about your certificate –

No one cares.

Emma   I care.

Jason   Yeh exactly.

Dean   Oi!

Paige   Shut up, Jason, you're so thick that's why you never get anything at school you're just so stupid.

Jason   WHAT?

Say that again.

Dean   Oi!

Jason   SHUT UP, YOU LITTLE BITCH.

Paige   YOU SHUT UP, JASON.

Dean   OI THAT'S ENOUGH.

Jason *sits silently for the rest of the meal*.

Silence.

Dean   Come on, eat. So?

Paige   Nothing, it's just a piece of paper.

Emma   Still . . .

Paige   I don't really need it.

Emma   You should be proud of yourself.

Paige   Yeah.

Dean   Well done, love.

Pause.

Paige   I'm cold.

Dean *gives his jumper to* **Paige**.

Dean   Come on, eat up.

Pause. **Emma** *passes her plate to* **Dean**.

Emma   Do you want the rest of this?

Dean   No, you should have it.

Emma   I've had enough.

Dean   Thank you.

It'll be alright, babe.

Colin *enters.*

Colin   Feast. Everyone alright?

Dean   Yeah we're all fine thank you.

Colin   You've got your bidding number then?

Dean   Yeah there's been a mix-up, just a couple of things to sort out / but all fine

Colin   Tell me about it.

Who is your caseworker?

Emma   Angela /

Colin   Harrison? Twat.

Emma   Yeh, do you know her then?

Colin   Yeh we've had her for ages.

Emma   How long you been in here?

Colin   About twelve, yeh getting on for about twelve months I suppose yeh.

Emma   That's not possible though is it they put you here / they're.

Colin   Well, it is.

Dean   No, it's six weeks maximum by law that's what they said to us.

Colin   Alright mate yeh.

Emma   No, no, he's right, it's against the law, you can't be in /

Colin   Yeh al / right.

Emma   No mate / we were in them offices like a week ago mate yeh so.

Colin   Alright love, it's the council though isn't it, it's the council, they can do what the fuck they want you know.

Emma   Yeh, but hold on.

Colin   NO, NO, NO,just cos you're pregnant, right, DON'T MEAN YOU CAN'T GET FUCKED.

Pause   Sorry. I didn't mean like, d'ya know what I mean, I didn't mean like.

A time. **Emma** *stands and goes towards the bedroom.*

Colin   Sorry.

Emma   I mean obviously *your* circumstances are different. I think our situation will change when we / actually get a chance to speak to someone.

Colin   Totally different mate.

Emma   So, it's fine.

Dean   Emma.

Pause. She exits to her room upstage.

Colin *sits downstage in one of the audience-area seats.*

Dean   Do you want to go to the park?

Jason   No.

Paige   Yeah.

Dean   Go and get your coat then.

Paige *goes into the bedroom then re-enters.*

Colin   Sorry / I just.

Dean   Yeah, it's fine, just want to get some / air.

Colin   Yeh, no worries mate, no worries.

Dean *and* **Paige** *exit.*

Colin *goes to the family bedroom and listens.*

He knocks on the door.

Colin   Alright.

Emma   Yeh /

Colin   Listen no I just wanted to apologise ab / out.

Emma   Yeh no look right it's fine it's alright.

Colin   Ah fucking hell man.

During the following **Barbara** *enters and then is there overhearing.*

Emma   Thank you for the apology /

Colin   Yeh no /

Emma But you have to see where I'm coming from. We are trying to stay positive in here, so yeh you've been here for like a year but that doesn't necessarily mean that we are going to be here for a year?

So for you to be bringing that, well, negative energy into the communal area and like you know like when people try to, maybe unintentionally, you know well I.

Colin Yeh.

No don't / like / it's bad karma.

Pause. They stand in silence.

I'm / sorry, love /

Emma Yeh no / right /

Colin Yeh.

(*To* **Barbara**.) Y'alright? What?

Barbara .

Colin D'you want me to wash your hair?

Barbara No.

Colin No?

Barbara No.

Colin No? You like it when I wash your hair.

Barbara .

Colin Go on, you like it when you're nice and clean.

Barbara Use the fairy.

Barbara *stops outside the family bedroom and looks at* **Colin**.

Colin What? Fuck you then, I'm only trying to make you happy.

Barbara Oh, no, no. No.

Colin Fuck.

They cross to kitchen. **Colin** *runs warm water into a pan.*

Colin Nice that.
Come on then bab, over you come.
Lean over. You alright there?

Barbara Yeh.

Colin Are you ready? Ready?

Barbara Yeh.

Colin   Here it comes then.

He pours and she shrieks.

Barbara   Fucking fuck.

Gone down me neck.

Colin   Lean forward then you pillock.

Barbara   It's gone all down me neck.

Colin   You'll get a cold man.

Shall I use the fairy? *(He does)*.
You've got lovely hair ain't you, Mum?
D'ya want me to do your ears?

Barbara   No, get off.

Colin   Up you come then, up you come. You cold?

Barbara   Yeh.

Colin *runs another pan of water.*

Colin   Over you go then. Are you ready? Are you ready?

Barbara   Yeh.

He pours and she shrieks again.

Fucking hell.

Colin   Get it all clean.

Barbara   Squeaky.

Colin   Squeaky clean. Get it squeaky.

Up you come then.

Look at you. You're like a golden princess.

Pause.

Barbara   I love you.

Colin   I love you too, Mum.

Barbara   Yeah.

Get me a towel.

Tharwa *enters. Crosses to the bathroom.*

Barbara   Yeah.

Get me a towel.

Colin   I'll use this.

He takes a tea towel from near the sink.

Barbara   Oh Colin, I need the.

Colin   OK OK.

He and **Barbara** *cross to the loo.* **Colin** *bangs on the door.*

Colin   Excuse me! Excuse me!

Can you hurry up please, my mum's.

Tharwa   I just come in give me five minutes please.

Colin   Can't last that long.

Sorry it's for my mum.

Tharwa   Don't push the door.

Colin   I'm not pushing the door.

Mate, hurry up.

Cue family argument in bedroom with **Jason** *overheard.*

There are regular interruptions between the two scenes so that in some way they feel like one musical piece. **Colin** *is aware that there are people that could emerge at any moment to this scene.*

Colin (*to* **Tharwa**)   Can you just hold it if you're only having a piss?

Tharwa *leaves the bathroom, goes to exit.*

Colin   Thank you, sorry.

Emma   Do you think it's OK to talk like that to me to talk like that no it's not.

Jason   Shut up.

Colin   Do you want some wipes?

Barbara   No.

Colin   Are you sure you're going to get it properly clean.

Cos I don't want to clean the bed again.

Barbara   No you're alright.

Emma   You can't you're twelve.

You haven't got anything in life.

You're not allowed.

Jason   I don't give a fuck.

Emma   Yeh go on then /

Jason *walks out.*

Jason *and* **Colin** *look at each other.*

Jason *thinks about running out of the space and then changes his mind – he has nowhere to go but back into the room. He does.*

Colin   Do you want the talcum.

Barbara   Nooo.

Colin   Y'alright, Mum.

Barbara *emerges and they cross slowly to the room.*

Colin   Come on then, come on Princess.

I've got ya, I've got ya haven't I?

Emma *emerges to study at the table.*

Adnan *enters, hesitates a beat about going to the sink, apologises and goes back to the room.*

Pause.

Enter **Dean** *and* **Paige** *from the park.*

Dean   It's raining.

Emma   Go and get dried off, love.

Paige *goes to get dried off in the room. They wait.*

Emma   You alright?

Dean   Yeh I'm alright, you?

Emma   Yeh I'm a bit freaked out by them being there a year . . .

Dean   Yeh but it's not going to be us is it?

Paige *goes into the bedroom.*

Emma   Well what happened then?

Dean   I told you.

Emma   Have you told them everything that's happened to us in the last six weeks ? You've been there /

Dean   I TOLD THEM EVERYTHING – I've been there all day.

Emma   I'm not attacking you, Dean.

Dean   You ARE attacking me sorry I'm tired I'm also tired.

Emma   I'm not denying you are tired I just I wasn't there I've been in this room ALL DAY with like, all these people, and it's doing my head in and I just want to check /

Dean   I told you I'VE GOT IT and it's going to be fine you just think about the baby and / stay calm.

Emma   I DON'T WANT MY BABY TO BE BORN HERE.

Dean   I DON'T WANT MY BABY TO BE BORN HERE EITHER.

Jason *enters.*

Jason   I want to call Mum.

Dean   Well you can't.

Jason   Why?

Emma   Dean!

Dean   Sorry, mate, in a minute yeh.

Jason (*under his breath*)   Fucksakes.

He goes back into the bedroom.

Dean   I'll call the number on Monday.

Emma   We're low on food.

Dean   I'll sort it, I promise Emma I . . . Love . . .

Emma   No. Please. Sorry.

She takes his phone.

I need to call the council office.

Dean   Well the office is closed /

Emma   I need to call them right now /

Dean   There's no point, they've got nothing to do with it, it's the job centre now so you're just wasting your time.

Emma   Go / Go.

Dean   You're wasting my minutes as well.

He exits to the bedroom.

Emma *tries to make a call.*

Emma   Hi, Angela, my name is Emma Lowell, my partner Dean Gray came in to see you today. I just wanted to check in and see if everything is alright cos obviously we filled in all the paperwork with you and were hopeful to be moving towards getting a bidding number . . . I just want to make sure there hasn't been a mix-up because I know you said you'd be helping us.

Maybe we can have a quick catch-up sometime, I think you've got all my details, hope you're well, OK, thank you, bye.

Tharwa *enters during the call. She goes to wash a mug in the sink.*

Emma   Excuse me. I think that's our mug.

Tharwa   Are you sure?

You're not right.

Emma   Sorry I know what my mug looks like.

Tharwa   Go and check your stuff. Since you arrived you looked at me badly. This mug been here for eight months.

Emma   I haven't done anything to disrespect you yeh that's not the way I behave.

Tharwa   You looking to me not nice.

Emma   Can you listen to me for one minute. I know what my shit looks like.

Tharwa   I do not like this. I do not like this at all.

Emma   Look, it's my stuff.

Can you not touch our stuff cause you don't wash it properly.

Tharwa   You are very rude. This is not your mug.

I do not like this.

They talk over each other. **Tharwa** *exits.*

Emma   Unbelievable.

She knocks at her bedroom door.

Dean   Who is it?

Emma   Dean!

She goes in.

Short pause.

Jason *comes out, sits alone at the table.*

Silence.

He starts rapping to himself quietly – he thinks he's alone. He checks it first and then he does a small part of a song by the rapper Baseman.

Enter **Adnan**.

Adnan   Hi.

Jason   Hi.

They don't know how to communicate. They stop.

Adnan *slowly does a bit of rapping to tease* **Jason**.

Adnan   Yo let it go.

Jason *is embarassed.*

Adnan *exits.*

Jason *alone.*

Blackout.

Act Two

Scene One

Monday morning.

The following scene is a kind of 'ballet' in which the staging carries a lot of the energy.

Actions happen very fast and over the top of each other.

Barbara *is on stage.* **Dean** *is sitting in the audience area on the phone.*

She's looking up at the branch.

Barbara   Fucking stupid cow.

Emma *walks in.* **Barbara** *notices that* **Emma** *is looking at her. She freezes.*

Barbara   .

Emma   .

Babe, Paige needs you to help her in the room.

Dean   I'm still on hold.

Emma   Well Paige needs you.

She goes into the loo. **Dean** *goes into the bedroom.*

Adnan *walks in.* **Barbara** *is scared.*

He puts his stuff in the fridge, moving a few things.

Barbara *thinks about saying something but doesn't.*

Colin *comes in. He's about to go out (he has been threatening to do so all day). He looks at the fridge.*

Barbara   Col . . .

Colin   Scuse me, mate? Scuse me, mate? You alright, mate? You alright? Sorry. You using the middle shelf there? The middle shelf? That shelf's ours. Sorry. Can you use the other shelf? No room.

Adnan   Sorry.

He moves everything.

Colin   Use the other shelf, use the smaller shelf, is that OK? Is that alright, mate? Cheers.

(*To* **Barbara**.)   You got that letter?

Barbara   Just give me a minute.

He goes into the room.

Paige *comes in. Moment of solitude.*

Barbara   Hello.

Paige   Hello.

Barbara   Are you going to school?

Paige   Yeh.

Barbara (*fast*)   I was always so upset at school I don't know why.

Paige   .

Barbara   I'm sure you prefer being at school don't you?

I wanted to give you something, hang on.

Enter **Dean**.

Barbara   I'll get it.

Barbara *exits.*

Emma *enters from the loo. She goes into the bedroom.*

Paige   I'm hungry.

Dean   D'you want some toast?

He puts the phone on to loudspeaker and leaves it in the audience seating area on a free chair.

Don't touch that.

Emma *enters with her coat on.*

Emma   Dean, I'm going to the hospital.

Dean   I thought you were taking Paige to school.

Emma   No I already told you I have to go today. Paige, I'll see you later, have a good day.

She exits.

Dean *goes into the bedroom.*

Adnan *goes into the space. He sees* **Paige** *looking lost and kind of dances to the muzak for a second to amuse her.*

She smiles at him. He goes out.

Jason *comes out.*

Dean *re-enters. He makes toast for* **Paige**.

V/O (*on phone*) Right I can confirm that you have been referred for a sanction due to non-attendance at a job-coaching session.

Dean *picks up the phone.*

Dean What do you mean you're sanctioning us, what is that?

What, sorry, you can't just cut my money for missing one job-centre appointment on the day I was being evicted. Sorry I said at the time – I was stood in the council building with my children and all our stuff on the day we were being evicted and our caseworker Angela Harrison and she made it clear that this would be passed onto the appropriate people –

But you can't do this to us. My partner is about to have a baby and we need to eat and pay rent. How is this legal? You can't punish us for doing what we were told to do.

I don't want to appeal online! Can I speak to your manager please?

Sorry, no, listen, listen, sorry I wasn't being rude, listen, listen, listen, no, no, sorry.

When can I go? That's in forty minutes. OK, I'll make it, I'll make it.

Hangs up. Bangs on the table.

FUCK.

A time. **Paige** *thinks about her options.*

Paige I want to go to school.

Dean You're not going today.

Paige I want to go to school.

Dean I know you do. I heard you but I haven't got time to take you to school, you'll have to come to the job centre with me.

Paige I want to go.

Dean I just said we aren't going.

Paige *can't deal with it so goes to the toilet to lock herself into it.*

Dean Paige.

Paige.

Paige.

Come out of the toilet.

Paige No because you keep shouting.

Dean I'm sorry, please come out of the toilet.

Paige, I've got to go.

Paige Fine.

Dean   OK. I'm going to call Emma and tell her to come back for you.

Paige   Fine.

Dean   Fine.

He tries to call **Emma***. Leaves a voicemail.*

Dean   Em, it's me. I'm sorry. You're going to have to come back to the B and B – Paige has locked herself in the toilet. Sorry. Just call me when you get this.

(*To* **Jason***.*)   Right you're going to have to stay and look after your sister.

Yes?

Yes?

Jason   Fine.

Dean   Right, thank you, Jesus, use your words, Christ.

I've got to go. Sorry.

Paige, stay with your brother OK?

Paige   Fine.

Dean   Alright, I'm sorry Paige, sorry.

Dean *exits.*

Jason *steps out of the bedroom, but retreats when he sees* **Barbara***.*

Barbara *enters. She looks in her bag.* **Colin** *follows.*

Colin   Right, I'm off then yeh?

Barbara   Here take this.

She gives him a letter.

Colin   Right, I'm going then yeh?

Barbara   Yeh.

Colin   Huh?

Barbara   Give us a kiss Col.

He does.

I'm so happy.

Colin   Just don't build your hopes up yeh?

Barbara   Oh no no.

Oh Col I hope.

Colin   Alright, I'm gonna do my best yeh?

I'm going then yeh?
Well shall I go then?
Well then go back in the room, stop being so weird man.

Exit **Colin**.

Paige *enters from the bathroom.*

Barbara   Oh here, I found the thing I was looking for. Can I give it to you?

Barbara *takes a crucifix off her neck and puts it round* **Paige***'s neck.*

Barbara   I feel like a little girl sometimes.

Paige *is trying to get away.* **Barbara** *sort of holds her back, either physically or just by some other means.*

Barbara   Hang on don't go.

Holds her back.

Sorry. Like my body . . . I've got this feeling in my body now like *life is there*! But I can't control my bum you know.

Can you get me a glass of water?

Paige *brings it to her.*

Jason *comes in.*

Jason   Paige.

Paige   One second.

Barbara   Maybe you can let me talk to you sometimes eh? Yeh? I'm so tired.

Jason   Paige, come back to the room.

Emma *has rushed back to look after* **Paige***.*

Emma (*through the doorway*)   Guys, sorry.

Your dad didn't tell me and he just called me now – are you OK?

Paige   Yeh.

Emma   So sorry. Thank you.

Barbara   We're going soon.

Emma   Yeh hopefully / we are too.

Barbara   My son's gone to the council.

Emma   My partner is / at the.

Barbara   He's got a doctor's letter. They promised us a place.

Emma *smiles.*

Emma   Excuse me.

She goes back to her room.

Barbara *waits a moment. She goes back towards her room then pauses outside it. She looks towards the doorway, where* **Colin** *will come through with news of her fate.*

Blackout.

Scene Two

Five hours later. The quiet before the storm.

Barbara *in the room; we can see her through the door in the light from the window.* **Adnan** *revealed on stage. He is watching a film on his phone, the final scene of* Billy Elliot *dubbed into Arabic.*

Emma *enters – she goes to wash up her mugs.*

Adnan   Billy. It's *Billy Elliot.*

They smile at each other.

Something kind passes between them. **Emma** *is about to speak to him.*

Tharwa *enters.*

Tharwa   I need to say something. The cup is yours. I just confused.

Emma   Yeah it is.

Tharwa   I didn't mean to make you stress. I'm really sorry for your baby.

Emma   Umm. It's OK.

Tharwa   I am also a mother, madam. My children are joining me soon.

Emma   Yeah – oh great.

Well thank you.

She goes back to the room. **Adnan** *and* **Tharwa** *alone.*

Adnan   Everything is OK?

Pause.

Tharwa   Yes. excuse me, where are you from?

Adnan   Syria.

Tharwa   Do you speak Arabic?

Adnan   Yes. My name is Adnan.

He stands up and places his hand on his chest, in the formal Arab style. She offers her hand for a handshake.

The following is all in Arabic.

Tharwa   Hello, my brother, I'm from Sudan.

They shake hands.

Adnan   Hello and welcome /

Tharwa   How are you /

Adnan   I'm fine /

Tharwa   Let me offer you tea.

Adnan   I have juice. Can I offer you some?

He crosses to get cups. She hesitates then sits. Silence as he brings cups. As he places cups.

Tharwa   No, thank you. In Sudan we drink this *fresh* from the tree, not from these cartons.

Adnan   But this is good actually!

Tharwa   In Sudan we have mangos, lemons, all growing around /

Adnan   *Mashallah* (God willed it).

Pause.

Tharwa   Did you hurt your foot?

Adnan   No, no, everything is OK.

Tharwa   In Sudan we say Syria is beautiful, we say Syria is beautiful /

Adnan   Yes . . .

Tharwa   It will get better *Inshallah* (God willing).

Adnan   *Inshallah.*

Tharwa   *Inshallah.*

Pause.

In Sudan we just love Syrian soap operas!

Adnan   Oh really?

Tharwa   We really love Mohanned and . . .

Adnan   Not 'Mohanned and Noor'?!

Tharwa   Yes 'Mohanned and Noor', exactly! Honestly I love it! I watched it all the time with my family. Honestly we loved it.

Adnan   But 'Mohanned and Noor' is actually Turkish.

Tharwa   Oh really?!

She laughs and covers her smile with her scarf.

Adnan   Yes, it's only dubbed into Syrian Arabic /

Tharwa   It's really Turkish? I really thought it was Syrian.

Paige *enters and goes to the fridge. She runs back to the room.*

Tharwa   That little girl is beautiful!

Adnan   Yes . . . What's the name of the woman in that room?

Tharwa   Emma, her name is Emma, she lives with those children, they are nice actually. But the guy in that room, I don't like him he scares me.

Pause.

But *Elhamdullah* (Thank God).

Long silence where she thinks about her own family.

Elhamdullah.

Silence.

Adnan   I'm happy to have met you.

Tharwa   Me too.

He gets up to go.

Take care of yourself.

Adnan   Yes.

Tharwa   Take care of yourself.

Adnan   And you, goodbye.

Tharwa   Goodbye.

They end the conversation. **Adnan** *leaves.* **Tharwa** *is left alone again in the common room.*

Tree hits skylight.

Barbara *enters.*

Barbara   I like to look at that tree.

Yeh.

We had one like that at home.

I want to take Colin back to the sea, where I was brought up.

Tharwa   I miss the River Nile too.

Paige *goes to the bathroom.* **Emma** *follows after with a toilet roll.*

Tharwa *smiles.*

Enter **Colin**.

Barbara   How did it go?

Colin   Fine yeh.

Barbara   Did you show her the letter?

Colin   Yeah.

Barbara   How long? One week two weeks?

Colin   There's no housing.

Barbara   But did you give them the doctor's letter . . .

Colin   Made no difference, Mum.

Barbara   But.

She sits.

Colin   .

Barbara (*barely audible*)   Maybe I should go back to that home and die.

Colin   What?

Barbara   I just thought we could've moved back to the coast.

Colin   Mum, stop talking about the seaside, we only went there once.

Pause.

Barbara   A cup of tea?

Colin   No fuck it.

Emma *and* **Paige** *leave the bathroom and go into their bedroom.*

Colin   There's nothing for us, Mum. I was there five hours, she only gave me five minutes. Sat behind a piece of glass. She said they haven't got anything, they're still assessing our case . . .

Barbara   And?

Colin   She upset me, Mum.

I got upset with her.

He goes to the room.

Emma *enters.*

Barbara *waits.*

Emma   You OK?

Barbara Yeh.

Enter **Adnan**.

Adnan You're a student? Hi.

Emma Hi. Yeh. Trying to be.

Adnan What?

Emma It's massage and wellness therapy. What about you?

Adnan Yes, I was a primary school teacher.

Enter **Dean** *carrying large shopping bags that seem used already.*

Emma Dean, when did you go shopping?

Paige *runs to* **Dean***,* **Jason** *follows. They attack the shopping bags.*

Dean Hold on, hold on, wait for dinner will you?

Paige Is there anything I can eat now? I'm hungry.

She picks out a pack of mince pies.

These?

Dean No, we're going to save those for Christmas.

Paige But I'm hungry.

Dean Here you go.

He gives her a packet of cornflakes. **Jason** *pulls out a packet of biscuits.*

Dean Don't just eat the biscuits, take them to the room.

Jason *takes the two bags into the bedroom.*

Emma You only got tinned vegetables?

Dean I had to go to the food bank.

Emma But I thought you said we'd be fine you were / seeing them today to sort it out.

Dean I know but it's what I had to do.

They've cut our money for a while. And we have to stay here till they start it up again.

Emma But we've done nothing wrong – they're just punishing /

Dean I know, Emma – I'm going back there tomorrow.

Silence. **Emma** *goes towards the kitchen.*

Paige Is everything OK, Dad?

Dean Everything's fine, babe. Don't worry about anything OK?

Emma *begins to heat up some soup.*

Dean *opens his backpack and pulls out some Christmas decorations.*

Dean   Hey, look what I got for Christmas.

Paige   Cool.

Dean   Yeah? Do you want to come and help me put them up?

Paige   Yeah.

Dean   Come on then. Where shall we put it?

Paige   Up high.

They do so with some excitement and then it fades to something simpler. The cold returns.

Dean (*to* **Jason**)   You going to help?

Jason   I'm really tired.

Dean   We're going to eat soon.

Pause.

Jason *throws some tinsel over the bunk bed.*

Right, now come and do one properly please.

Jason *puts tinsel around the bedroom door frame.* **Dean** *and* **Paige** *hang a star.* **Jason** *returns to sit on the bed, putting music on the iPad.*

Dean   Hey.

I'm sorry I shouted.

Paige.

I'm sorry I shouted, Paige.

Paige   It's OK, Dad.

Dean   I promise when we sort this out I'll take you to McDonald's.

Or Burger King.

Paige   McDonald's.

Dean   Yeh?

What'll you have?

Paige   I'll have a Happy Meal and some nuggets.

Dean   Yeah?

Paige   And ketchup and.

Chips.

Dean   Whatever you want.

Paige   When are we going to get a house, Dad?

Dean   Soon, promise.

Right, come on, mate.

Jason *comes over.*

Emma *pours the soup into bowls.*

Dean   Thank you, Emma.

They eat in silence.

A long silence. Just the sound of the family eating soup.

Paige *looks over at the Christmas decorations.*

Paige   Are we staying here for Christmas, Dad?

Dean   Come on, eat your soup.

Long pause. **Barbara** *wanders over to the sink. Takes a tablet with a glass of water.*

Jason   Thanks.

He exits to the room.

Paige   I'm still hungry.

Dean   Do you want some more soup?

Paige   I want pudding.

Barbara   I've got something for you.

Dean   No, you're alright.

Paige   I want it.

Dean   No, Paige.

Barbara   I'll get it.

Dean   No, honestly it's OK.

Barbara *exits. He clears the table.*

Dean   Come to the room?

Emma   .

Dean *goes to the room.*

Dean   Em?

Emma   Yeh coming.

You going to get ready for bed, Paige?

She goes into the room, leaving **Paige** *alone. She turns the lights off.*

Paige *sits alone, in silence, for a short while.*

The sound of the tree on the roof. She wanders towards the tree in the darkness and then stands under the skylight. Suddenly a drop of water falls from the roof and hits her. She jumps back in alarm but then slowly comes forward again and collects the raindrops falling through the roof into her outstretched palms.

Blackout.

Act Three

Scene One

Some days later, but not many. The day of the school nativity.

Lights up on **Jason** *sitting outside the bedroom with his iPad on. After a time,* **Paige** *enters practising 'Away in a Manger'.*

Jason   What the fuck are you doing?

Paige   Practising.

You need to practise too, Jason.

Jason   No.

Paige   You have to, you promised you'd do it.

Jason   I'm not doing it.

Paige   I'll get your costume?

Jason   I don't want a costume.

Paige   Say your lines?

She gives a piece of paper to him.

Say them, Jason.

Jason   First Shepherd. 'And there were shepherds living out in the fields nearby' /

Paige   Do it properly, Jason.

Jason   'keeping watch over their flocks at night. An angel of the Lord appeared to them and they were terrified' /

Paige   / terrified.

(Sings.) Away in a manger, no crib for a bed . . .

Jason *puts music on the iPad.*

Paige   Jason, turn that off. Jason. Jason, stop it.

Fuck you, Jason

She gives up and goes to the bedroom in a huff.

Barbara *emerges.* **Jason** *turns off the music.* **Barbara** *goes to the sink but then changes direction and stops in the middle of the room.*

She defecates on the floor. **Jason** *sits silently. She keeps walking to the toilet. There is a puddle of faeces on the floor.*

At the toilet door:

Barbara Col! Col!

Colin *emerges and goes to help her.*

Jason *goes to the kitchen.*

Barbara I'm sorry I'm sorry I'm sorry. (*Cries.*)

Jason *knocks at the door.*

Jason Emma! Emma!

The old woman shat on the floor.

Emma Excuse me!

Colin *and* **Barbara** *ignore her.*

They talk in the toilet, inaudible, sounds of him getting her changed and cleaned.

Barbara *is crying.*

Emma My kids wanna play out here do you just wanna clean it up.

Please! Please just.

Excuse me.

FUCK.

She gets cleaning stuff and starts cleaning.

Barbara *comes out,* **Paige** *comes out.*

Paige Ugh ugh sick.

Barbara Fuck off! FUCK OFF.

Paige *goes back into the bedroom.*

Emma Is that my dressing gown?

Colin Sorry it was hanging behind the door. I . . .

Emma I don't fucking want it now you can keep it.

Long pause. As he's out of room she goes to pick up the bin and returns to cleaning.

He emerges with the dressing gown and gives it to her – it dangles over the faeces, and accidentally some gets on it.

Emma Are you mental?

Colin Huh?

Emma The floor's not clean mate.

Colin No.

Emma *goes mad and starts taking out everything that's happened till now in the play out on him.*

Emma What am I going to do with a dressing gown that's got your mum's shit all over it? I said I didn't want it so give it to your fucking mum.

She slaps him in the face.

Pause – like she's seen herself.

Colin *breaks down.*

Colin   Please don't hit me. Please.

I am sorry.

He puts the dressing gown on a chair and exits.

Emma *cleans up, putting the dressing gown in the bin bag. It takes a period of time and she's nearly vomiting as she does it. She goes to put the bin bag outside.*

Colin *emerges to apologise.* **Emma** *returns.*

Emma   I'm so sorry, I'm sorry, I'm so so sorry, I'm sorry.

Colin   Can I touch it?

Emma   Sorry?

Colin   The baby.

Emma   No . . . I . . .

Colin   Please.

He slowly moves towards her.

Emma   Careful.

He touches her belly. They look at each other. Slowly they begin to smile. He cries.

Silence.

Barbara *calls from the bedroom then enters.*

Barbara   Col?

Col?

Colin.

I need to speak to you.

Colin   Not now please.

Barbara   It's important, love.

Colin   Just give me a minute Mum.

Barbara   I just need to speak to you /

Colin   Just leave me alone, Mum.

Dean *enters and crosses past* **Barbara** *and* **Colin** *to the bedroom.*

Colin (*to Dean*)   You alright mate?

Barbara   Col, I just need.

Colin   I've wiped your fucking arse for you!

I'm so sorry. I'm so sorry Mum.

Dean *goes into the room.*

He exits.

Barbara   I love you.

Barbara *goes towards her room.*

Barbara   Do forgive me.

I don't know what I'm doing.

Emma   It's alright.

Barbara *exits.* **Emma** *goes to the bedroom door. She stops and sits outside the room.*

Dean *enters.*

Dean   Em, Jason told me what happened. I'm sorry /

Emma moves to the table.

Pause. **Dean** *goes to the bedroom door.*

Emma   I love you, Dean.

I just don't know who is going to help us.

Dean   I'm trying my best.

Emma   Dean. Come here.

Dean *goes to* **Emma.**

Emma   Are we going to be OK?

They hug and kiss.

Dean   I love you.

Paige *comes in. She is dressed in an angel costume ready for her nativity play.*

Barbara *enters.* **Adnan** *enters with his bags.*

Paige   Dad, Dad, look at my costume.

Dean   You look beautiful.

He and **Emma** *go towards the bedroom.*

Dean   Oh, you're off are you?

Adnan   Yes.

Dean   Good luck then.

The family exit to their bedroom.

Adnan *crosses to exit.*

Barbara   Bye.

Adnan   Bye.

Adnan *exits.*

Silence.

Colin *comes back. He goes towards* **Barbara***.*

Colin   I'm sorry, Mum.

Barbara   You'll be alright when I'm gone.

When I'm gone you'll be dancing.

Colin   I'll have a fucking party.

Barbara   You'll get a job maybe, find a girl.

Pause.

Col, I'm going to die.

Colin   We're all going to fucking die.

They laugh.

As he walks back to the room, barely audible:

Love you Mum.

He exits.

Pause.

Enter **Paige***,* **Jason***,* **Dean** *and* **Emma***.* **Jason** *is dressed as a shepherd.*

Barbara   Goodbye, little angel.

Paige   I've got my costume.

The family exit, **Dean** *trailing behind.*

Barbara   Could I have a glass of water?

Dean   Yeh.

Barbara   Do you like water?

Dean   Do I like water? I have to like water.

Barbara   Do you like swimming in the sea?

Dean   I haven't been for a while.

Barbara   I like water. I used to swim in the sea and my dad would say look, look, Barbara!

Dean *is desperate to get away.*

Dean   Right yeh.

Barbara   Gorgeous.

Dean.

Barbara   I'm very sorry about what happened earlier.

Dean   Yeah well they're only little so it can't really happen again.

Barbara   I love being in water. Not like here.

I love Colin as much as the sea, as big as the sea. (*Laughs.*)

Dean   What?

Barbara   NOT LIKE 'ERE!

Silence.

Fucking Floyd Mattison.

I went to the sea once, I was running towards the sea and my dad he said oh look at Barbara go, and I jumped in and I was /

Dean   Yeh /

Barbara   swimming and I could see everyone looking at me.

. . . /

Dean   Yeh sorry I better.

Barbara   Love?

Dean   .

He's gone.

The tree hits the roof.

Barbara *gets up. She leaves her stick.*

She walks towards the audience, she is very frail.

She sees them; looks at them straight in the face.

She uses the audience to support her as she walks out of the theatre. Silence.

Tharwa *enters and makes a call in Arabic. Her young daughter answers.*

Tharwa   Tala, Tala, Mumma loves you.

Do you remember when I used to sing to you, doha doha?

She sings her a lullaby.

Suddenly, mid-verse:

Blackout.

Acknowledgements for *LOVE*

I would like to thank Louise Walker, Renée and all her family. Esther, Verna, Renata, Possy, Aso as well as all those who spent time with me and the team. Write for Life, Shelter, Z2K, Crisis. Bill Rashleigh, who set this all off, Natasha Jenkins, Josh Grigg, Marc Williams, Diyan Zora, Marcin Rudy, Cathleen McCarron, Kev McCurdy, Emily Seekings, Fran Miller, Jane Suffling, Jo Nield, Ian Farmery, Nyasha Gudo.

Rufus Norris, Ben Power, Dominic Cooke, Roxana Silbert, thank you for your wisdom, support and friendship and for pushing me forward. Emily McLaughlin and all the team at the New Work Department at the National Theatre, where this play was developed, nurtured and loved, Stuart Rogers, Tessa Walker and the whole arts team at The REP, Peter Brook and Marie-Hélène Estienne, Margaret Zeldin, Finbar Mostyn-Williams.

Foreword to *Faith, Hope and Charity*

Lemn Sissay

It's all growth. I was a new-born baby when The Authority stole me from my mother. They renamed me so that I would be untraceable. Then they gave me to foster parents who trained the words 'mummy' and 'daddy' from my mouth and told me I was theirs forever. Twelve years later they put me into an institution and said they would never visit me. They never did. They stole my ability to form elegant sentences and memory fell to bits. I lost everyone and everything I had ever known.

From twelve to seventeen The Authority held me in four different institutions. The fourth was a prison (for children) which The Authority called an assessment centre. I was under surveillance twenty-four hours a day. I was strip searched. I was marched down corridors in size order with the others. I was locked in a dormitory each night by the Night Watchman. I heard screams when boys were dragged into the padded cell. It was known as The Quiet Room. You may ask what I did to deserve this treatment. I asked myself the same question.

The majority of children leave the 'care' system not begging for pity, not wanting to burden others with *the story*. We left 'care' as shell-shocked silent witnesses. Who would believe us anyway? Sorry. I'm not saying you wouldn't believe me. We enter the world of adulthood. We try to love and be loved though many of us find love. Difficult. We try to be open though as children we were forced *by strangers* to shut down. There's a bird trapped in the roof of the community hall and there's nothing we can do about it.

Adulthood. We are not great at birthdays but we try to celebrate birthdays. We hope no-one else can see. We see others who are invisible. It's a sixth sense. We offer to set out chairs. We offer to teach choir or sing in it, or not. It's like a family atmosphere. We try to help others. We know what it is like to be helpless. We offer to prepare food. Adulthood: Court cases and Christmas, Valentine's Day and spring, puddles and petitions, faith and fear, happiness and hope, children and charity. We say sorry for things we haven't done.

The Authority pretends to be a different person than the one which came into our lives when we were children. In this way The Authority is sociopathic with anti-social personality disorder and double standards. Zero-hour contracts, funding withdrawn, Definitions by data, files hidden in cabinets and encrypted computer memory, blank-faced bailiffs and rigged assessments are its darker 'challenging' personality traits. There's a leak in the ceiling. I'm glad you're here. Mind the water. Have a seat. It's all growth. Yeh.

Faith, Hope and Charity

Second edition as of 17 June 2021

The original production of *Faith, Hope and Charity* opened at the National Theatre's Dorfman Theatre on 17 September 2019 with the following cast and creative team:

Ensemble	Nathan Armarkwei-Laryea
Mason	Nick Holder
Tala	Kamia Hunte
	Ayomide Mustafa Ashanti
	Prince-Asafo
Carl	Dayo Koleosho
Beth	Susan Lynch
Hazel	Cecilia Noble
Anthony	Corey Peterson
Marc	Bobby Stallwood
Tharwa	Hind Swareldahab
Bernard	Alan Williams

Director	Alexander Zeldin
Set and Costume Designer	Natasha Jenkins
Lighting Designer	Marc Williams
Movement Director	Marcin Rudy
Sound Designer	Josh Anio Grigg
Rehearsal Music Director	Laurie Blundell
Associate Director	Diyan Zora
Company Voice Work	Jeannette Nelson
Assistant Voice Coach	Victoria Woodward

Faith, Hope and Charity received its European Premiere at the Odéon Théâtre de l'Europe's Ateliers Berthier on 17 June 2021, with the following cast and creative team:

Beth	Lucy Black
Tala	Tia Dutt
Hazel	Llewella Gideon
Irene	Tricia Hitchcock
Carl	Dayo Koleosho
Anthony	Joseph Langdon
Sunny	Shelley McDonald
Mason	Michael Moreland
Bernard	Sean O'Callaghan
Marc	Bobby Stallwood
Leigh	Posy Sterling
Tharwa	Hind Swareldahab

Director	Alexander Zeldin
Set and Costume Designer	Natasha Jenkins

Lighting Designer	Marc Williams
Movement Director	Marcin Rudy
Sound Designer	Josh Anio Grigg
Rehearsal Music Director	Laurie Blundell
Associate Director	Josh Seymour
Associate Lighting Designer	Breandan Ansdell

Characters

Hazel, *late fifties-early sixties. The lead volunteer and cook.*
Mason, *mid forty. A new volunteer, recently taken over the choir.*
Bernard, *seventy. A local man.*
Beth, *late thirties. A mother whose daughter is being taken into care.*
Marc, *sixteen. Her son.*
Tharwa, *forty-ish. A woman from abroad, now living locally.*
Tala, *nine. Her daughter.*
Carl, *thirty. A local man who needs support.*
Anthony, *twenty. A local young man who is alone.*

Others, different local people who use the centre.
In this edition there are three additional community members (**Leigh**, **Sunny** *and* **Irene**)

Act One takes place at the end of November, the day of Beth's trial but also of Mason's first shift. It's the first lunch without Pete.

Act Two takes place at Christmas time. Just before Christmas.

Act Three takes place around Valentine's Day, just before the concert that is proposed in Act Two.

Act Four takes place at the very beginning of spring, March or April.

'.' marks a thought that doesn't become a word.

'/' marks an interruption that means the actors speak over one another.

Act One: November, the end of autumn

Scene One

We are in an old, dilapidated church hall. A community centre.

Above, there are vast windows, which provide most of the light, there was once a kind of stained glass painted windows, which have been replaced in the 1960–70s. Upstage, a kitchen area. On the wall – there are several children's drawings that are on yellowing paper, they have been there for fifteen to twenty years.

12.00.

There is a pot of stew on in the kitchen. It smells, wafting into theatre. An occasional drip from the ceiling.

Hazel *comes through the kitchen. She looks at the drip. Before she has a chance to go and get a bucket, her phone gets a message, she looks at it and goes out.*

Silence. After some more time, **Mason** *and* **Hazel** *re-enter and begin talking at the back.*

Hazel   Come in yeh /

Mason   Thanks yeh oh, OK?

Hazel   I'm just gonna get the stuff from the car? Can you put the tables and chairs out?

Mason   Oh.

Hazel   In like a triangle?

Mason   Right yeh. OK.

Beat, **Hazel** *goes.*

Mason *is alone, does the flyers, does the chairs.*

Mason   Do you need to come in?

Bernard   Yeh.

Mason   I'm Mason nice to meet you I'm running the / choir.

Bernard   Where's Pete?

Mason   No Pete's not been well mate. No . . . so I'm running the / choir yeh.

Bernard   I've come for the choir I'm looking forward / to it.

Mason   Oh yeah yeah I'm looking after the choir.

Bernard   I'm looking forward to it.

Mason   Oh good yeh I hope it's alright and that yeh cheers.

Silence.

Hazel?

She'll be back in a minute.

Yeh.

He laughs slightly. **Bernard** *wanders off into the back rooms.*

Mason   Oh I don't think you're supposed to go back there.

Mate? Yeh I?

Fuck.

He's gone.

Mason *lets him go and is a bit pointless now suddenly in the space.*

There is wind outside, the storm is only just beginning. He notices the wind, looks up to the window.

Silence.

Hazel *enters.*

Hazel   It might rain.

She has some shopping, he helps her with it.

He looks up out the window to the sky demonstrably, as if he hadn't just done this, maybe points. It's funny.

Mason   Oh.

I'll just put these out yeh?

Mason   Alright yeh no.

Hazel   You can /

Mason   Oh OK.

Child's painting falls off the wall.

Mason   Shall I /

Hazel   No I'll do it I've got /

Mason   Oh yeh sorry sorry.

But **Hazel** *goes over and puts it back up. She walks across the space and it takes her a long time* **Mason** *notices.*

Hazel   These have been here for years.

Mason   Right.

Well they've kept well /

Hazel   Yeh.

Mason   They must have grown up.

Hazel   Who.

Mason   The kids who did the drawing.

Hazel   Oh yes.

There used to be all sorts / of activities and.

Mason   Yeh?

Hazel   Drawing an / d art and.

Mason   Colouring in.

Do you want me to set that table up?

Hazel   Oh you'll need help with that.

Yeh.

There is an issue with the table how it folds.

Mason   No I've got it.

Hazel   No hang on you'll need help.

She helps him.

Mason   Sorry yeh.

Sorry.

Hazel   No it's fine that table is a bit heavy.

Mason   Yeh it's heavier than it looks.

Hazel   Oh yes you'd think the feet would move more like.

In that way.

Mason   Yeh exactly!

It's a bit warmer.

Hazel   It's good to have you here . . with Pete being ill / and that.

Mason   Oh no yeh . . . I want to / like or whatever is needed.

Hazel   Yeh /

Mason   Sorry.

Hazel   Are you here all day then or just for the / choir?

Mason   Yeh Pete said it'd be good to do the choir and then you know help you out with the cooking and that /

Hazel   Right yes OK. Yeh he said you are musical /

Mason   I helped out in the kichens, yeh actually and.

I know Marcus.

Hazel   Which Marcus?

Beat.

Mason   Your son.

Hazel   My Marcus.

Mason   Yeh I was like fuck cos I left round here when we was growing up I moved around a lot in my childhood yeh but fuck I would ha / sorry. . .

Hazel   Oh. OK.

Mason   Yeh . . .

He's doing alright isn't he though and what is it November now four months till he's out or something?

Beat.

Hazel   So how d'you know Pete?

Mason   Yeh Pete he was helping me re- re-adjust and things /

Hazel   Oh right.

Mason

Beat

I wouldn't be here without Pete (*laughs*)

But yeh, it's all growth isn't it.

Short pause. **Hazel** *not sure how to react.*

Anyway thanks for having me and letting me . . . you won't. . . .

Thanks from the bottom of my heart.

Hazel   No it's OK.

Pete'll be back in a couple /

Mason   Oh is that what they've said that?

Hazel   Yeh a couple weeks he'll be on his feet / and yeh.

Mason   Yeh.

You gonna join the choir?

Hazel   I haven't sung in years. No.

Beat.

Mason *laughs, realises it's weird to be laughing. Stops.*

Hazel *goes to the kitchen.*

Mason *comes in.*

Hazel   Oh, you coming in?

Mason (*Smiling.*)   Yeh (*gotta get stuck in*).

Hazel   You can hang your bag up?

Mason   I've got my life in there I never take it off.

Hazel   You can start with that bag.

Hazel *and* **Mason** *are in the kitchen rummaging through what is obviously donations.*

Hazel   People always donate tins.

Mason   Shall I put some fruit out and that.

Hazel   We don't have enough to go round.

Mason   Right.

There's a sound above.

Hazel   Oh no.

That's another bird.

Mason   Where what in / the.

Hazel   In the roof yeh.

Poor thing. Can't get out.

Can you go up there?

Mason   Oh I'm not good with heights.

Hazel   Can you put out the biscuits yeah / help yourself if you want one.

Mason   Oh no not me.

Mason *goes back out, starts laying out the stuff, he's feeling useful.*

Oh there's a bloke here sorry.

Hazel   Where is he?

Mason   He went back to that room you said not to /

Hazel   Bernard! It's Bernard!

She is already gone.

Mason *sits in the audience.*

Hazel   Bernard!

There's a damp problem in there.

The council said we're not supposed to go in there OK?

Bernard   Sorry.

Mason   Sorry I didn't.

Hazel   It's OK /

Mason

Beat.

Hazel   Bernard sit there OK love.

Lunch won't be long.

Beat.

Mason   I'll put these out.

Sorry!

Bernard *goes to the toilet, as he does* **Mason** *begins laying out the toys.*

Hazel   OK.

Short silence. **Mason** *puts out the toys.*

Mason   Oh I meant to say like.

I know obviously people here will be coming with.

Issues and things / and I.

Hazel   No.

Mason   I just want you to know I have experience and so I'm happy to help /

Hazel   No / yeh?

Mason   I, yeh to give back?

Sorry does that / make sense?

Hazel   No right. Yeh I mean thanks and you know it's great you're doing the choir and that's / great.

Mason   Great / no I got my flyers . . .

Hazel   Right and people will come to you at first / so maybe just focus on.

Mason   Totally. / I, I.

Hazel   Because but I mean there are some people who have some vulnerable situations and stuff going on here and?

Mason   Yeah.

Tharwa *has come in with* **Tala** *in the corner.*

Hazel   Like my friend she's going through a nightmare with social services at the moment / and with her kid and.

Mason   Right ok ok yeh / obviously.

Hazel   It being your first shift I think maybe yeh? You know. . . but the choir and / the chairs.

Mason   The chairs are a pleasure.

Hazel   Yeah cos people really need the food, so.

Beat.

Mason   It's all growth.

Enter **Tharwa**, *forties, and* **Tala** *who is nine years old.*

Tharwa   Hello.

Beat.

I am here for the 'lunch?'

Hazel   Hello, welcome.

She comes round.

Tharwa   At 1 o'clock?

Hazel   Yes! Yes that's us. Welcome.

Lunch won't be long.

Beat. **Tharwa** *doesn't know if she can wait here.*

You can wait here / though.

Tharwa   Thank you. Thank you.

Hazel   There's a play area actually / over there.

Tharwa   Oh / thank you.

Mason   Does she want some squash?

Tala   Yes. Thanks.

Tala *drinks squash. Beat. They settle down.* **Bernard** *comes out of the toilet.*

Bernard   I'm looking forward to the choir.

Mason   Great. See you in a bit yeh.

Tharwa (*in Arabic*)   Come here, Tala.

Tala   But I'm thirsty.

Tala *walks over to the table and sits with* **Tharwa**.

*Another community member (***Leigh***) wanders in, who is there for the lunch, she smiles at* **Hazel**. *First time she is there. They are greeted in simple way but don't respond, or just nod.*

Mason *wanders back to the kitchen.*

Bernard   I'll sit here yeh OK I'll sit here.

Tharwa (*in Arabic*)   Look Tala there's a choir.

Tharwa *looks at the choir flyer on the table,* **Bernard** *approaches when he sees this.*

Bernard   There's a choir.

Tharwa   Thank you.

Bernard   There's a choir after the lunch.

It's good /

Tharwa   Thank you.

Bernard   I like to sing I do I'm not much good but I have a go you know yeh?

Tharwa   Sorry . . .

Pause.

Bernard   I'm not very good at it but I have a go you know.

I did do some singing actually but the problem is I can never remember the lines.

Tharwa   That's fine.

Bernard   He's doing it, this guy he's the choir master.

Mason   You're / welcome.

Bernard   I can't remember the lines / that's my problem but I got very bad schooling!

Hazel   Bernard

Bernard   WHEN I WAS AT SCHOOL THEY WERE IMPATIENT WITH ME, THEY WERE. BUT I TRIED MY / HARDEST.

Tharwa   Excuse me yeah.

Beat. **Tharwa** *looks away.*

Bernard   But loved school I did. I'd go back there now in a flash.

Tharwa   Excuse me /

Enter **Carl**.

Hazel   Hi Carl.

Carl   Hi Hazel.

Hazel   Nice to see you.

Carl   Nice to see you too.

Bernard   Hi Carl.

Carl   Hi.

Tala *is sitting in the play area but refusing to play.*

Hazel   Do you want to go take a seat.

Carl *moves over.*

Carl   Where do I sit?

Hazel   Here love.

Carl   Oh that chair.

Bernard   I'm not a good singer but / I'll have a go.

Hazel   Where's your carer?

Carl   She had to go.

Hazel   Tea?

Carl   Yeah.

Mason   Milk and. . . .

Carl   Four.

Bernard   You here for the choir.

Carl   I'm here for the lunch.

Tala   I'm / hungry! /

Tharwa *gives* **Tala** *a biscuit. She goes to sit in the play area. She finds the toys unappealing.*

Bernard (*to* **Leigh**)   Would you like a flyer?

Leigh *turns away goes on their phone.* **Hazel** *takes* **Carl** *to his usual seat. In this moment of movement there is something else sonically – a noise from outside caused by* **Beth**. **Mason** *notices.*

Enter **Beth** *and* **Marc** *following her.*

She runs into the kitchen and hugs **Hazel**.

Hazel   Hi!

Beth   Hi, yeh.

Hazel   You look great.

Beth   Thanks, Hazel / I'm I hope I'm I, yeh.

Hazel   Go and sit down there and we'll chat after lunch OK /

Beth   Oh OK.

Hazel   Oh everyone this is Mason he is volunteering too now.

Mason   Hi.

Beth   Hi yeh.

Hazel   Mason has taken over the choir we used to have here.

He was a musician / is a musician /

Mason   No was!

Beth   .

Carl   Sorry.

Marc   Cool /

Beth   Marc's a musician.

Mason   Yeh anyway nice to meet you.

Tala *is still not playing, she's bored, the play area isn't inspiring her at the moment.*

Enter a young man, **Anthony**.

Hazel   Hello, welcome.

How are you?

Anthony   Good thank you yeh.

Hazel   What's your name?

Anthony   Euh.

Anthony.

Hazel   Sit anywhere you like.

Pause.

Anthony *and* **Marc** *notice each other.*

Tala   I'm hungry.

Tharwa *looks into the kitchen, doesn't say anything.* **Tala** *lies on the floor.* **Beth**'s *phone rings.*

Tharwa (*in Arabic*)   Don't lie on the floor. Come over here.

Beth *goes for a cigarette.*

Marc   You can't / is that Jason?

Beth   I've hung up on him. I'm going for a smoke.

Marc   Hurry up.

She leaves her phone there. As proof. Kisses him.

Anthony   Can I sit here?

Leigh   Yeh.

Silence.

Leigh *pushes the biscuit plate towards* **Anthony**.

Leigh   Do you like these?

Anthony   Don't mind them.

Anthony *eats the biscuits,* **Leigh** *watches him.*

Leigh   You hungry yeh.

Anthony   A little bit.

Tharwa *says to* **Tala** *to wait at the chair, and goes to make a tea.*

Anthony *gets a bowl.*

Hazel   In a minute, love.

Leigh *goes to pick up a bowl.*

Hazel   Food's ready. Make a nice queue please.

Lunch scene: people slowly line up at the hatch.

Tharwa *maybe jumps the queue.*

Tharwa (*in Arabic*)   Let's go OK come on Tala.

Tala   OK.

Carl   Thank God.

Marc *gets up, his phone is left on the table, he sees* **Bernard** *looking at it and then takes it.* **Bernard** *and* **Marc** *bump into each other.*

Bernard   Sorry.

Marc   Hi.

Bernard   No you go first.

Marc   No mate you.

Bernard   No you.

Marc *goes ahead, and then another community member (***Sunny***) enters and pushes in front of* **Bernard**, *who is now is last in the queue.*

An additional community member (**Irene***) has already entered by this point.*

Hazel   Do you want sauce?

Carl   Sorry.

Tharwa   Thank you.

Mason   Yeh ouf there you go.

Anthony   I like sauce yeh.

Marc   Thanks.

Mason   Alright mate.

Sorry? Oh thanks no yeh thank you mate thank you.

Tala *wanders towards the audience.*

Tala   Mum. Mum. Mum.

Tharwa (*in Arabic*)   Sit down don't go there.

Marc *brings two bowls to the table and goes to the garden to speak to* **Beth**.

Once they are all eating, a few long silent beats, around the food.

Hazel   Could you start on that washing up then?

Hazel *comes out and makes herself a tea.*

Hazel (*to super*)   Are you alright?

Hazel (*to* **Anthony**)   You from round here? You came here once with that girl what's her name.

Anthony   Yeh Charity /

Hazel   That's it she's got a pretty name. She alright?

Anthony   She's doing better yeh thank you /

Bernard   He's a poet.

Hazel   Oh you two know each other.

Anthony   Yeh we're in the same hostel.

He's exaggerating.

Bernard   No I'm not.

Pause.

Hazel *walks across the stage.*

Hazel (*to* **Beth**)   Beth come and eat.

Marc *re-enters.*

Marc   I don't know what she's doing.

Hazel *sits in the audience. She watches people eat.*

Hazel   How is my food, Bernard?

Bernard   Oh very good . . delicious.

Hazel   Thanks, Bernard, I'm glad.

This can draw a few smiles.

The rains starts up again outside.

Hazel   Oh it's raining.

Silence.

Hazel   Can't believe they closed the library because of a / bit of rain.

Bernard   Last year.

It was only a bit Pete said it was because / of.

Hazel   A bit of rain / yeh.

Bernard   Yeh / but the rain will be good for Pete's roses.

Hazel   They look good yeah.

Bernard   They are very nice.

Tharwa   Yes.

Quick beat.

Hazel (*to* **Leigh**)   Do you want some more food? (*Irene: Yeah*) Anthony wants some more he's a growing lad.

Leigh *goes to get food, as does* **Anthony** *and then* **Irene**.

Bernard *looks at* **Marc**.

Bernard   Where's your little sister that little girl that's with you all the time?

Marc   .

Bernard *looks at the mat.*

Bernard   She's normally running around in the garden she makes a mess actually /

Marc   Faith'll be back /

Bernard   Fa/ith.

Hazel (*getting him to keep quiet*)   Bernard, Bernard?

Tharwa (*in Arabic*)   Come and sit with mum.

Hazel   Why don't you sit with Anthony.

Anthony   It's / OK I.

Bernard   OK.

He does.

Hazel *takes a mug from* **Tharwa** *and* **Tala***'s table, she collects a few more things on the way and heads to the kitchen.*

Tala   Can I sing?

Tharwa (*in Arabic*)   Finish your food first.

Tala   I want to sing, Mum.

Tharwa (*in Arabic*)   Tala my darling, listen to mummy and finish your food.

Tala (*looking into bowl*)   Mum.

Bernard   So Hicham came into my room and he sat on my bed and he then told me he respected me.

Anthony   OK yeh.

Bernard   But then he thought it was funny so he pulled a toy gun on me and I said you know.

Anthony   Yeh / no.

Bernard   I said I'm going to smash it and it ended up on the wall the gun.

Hazel *goes back to the kitchen, as she does.*

Bernard   That friend of yours she keeps shouting on the top floor.

Anthony   Charity? She's not been well yeh leave her out of it.

Bernard   What's wrong with her?

Anthony   She's just.

Like she's got a lot she's trying to shake off.

Bernard   Do you sing?

Anthony   No.

Beth *enters:* **Beth** *runs into the kitchen to talk to* **Hazel** *(not all of this is heard perfectly).*

Marc   Mum?

Beth   Hazel? What I was thinking is maybe I should.

Hazel   Hi Beth one minute.

Hazel   Mason do you want to? Maybe if people have finished?

Mason   Oh OK.

Yeh.

Bernard   There used to be a choir.

Anthony   Cool, yeah.

Mason *comes out of the kitchen.*

Mason   I'll shall I?

Hazel   Yeh that'd be great?

As **Mason** *walks into the room.*

Tharwa (*in Arabic*)   After lunch we can go to the park.

Tala   But we'll miss the choir.

Tharwa (*in Arabic*)   But we will be late for home. Sit up properly please.

Tala   I am!

Below, the italicized speech is spoken underneath **Mason**.

Mason   Right yeh.

OK so yeh hi everyone – I'm Mason and I'm yeh I'm running a bit of a choir here?

Anthony   *Oh OK no thanks.*

Tharwa   *Tala finish your food and sit up.*

Hazel   *Can people listen oh sorry you want more (she serves the super more food).*

Exit **Irene** (*community member 1*).

Mason   I know there used to be something I know there used /

Marc   *Mum come back and yeh.*

Anthony   *See yah then Bernard yeh I'm gonna go I think.*

Mason   *Fair enough.*

Bernard   *Oh OK yeh I.*

Exit **Anthony**.

Mason   To be something here that yeh that well / just thought it's well it's nothing really just a chance for some of us to have a sing and that and yeh I guess a chance for growth?

Leigh   I'm not much of a singer.

Mason   Right so I've got my piano in the room back there –

Bernard *is off. Tala follows him.*

Mason   Right thanks, Bernard! There you go, on the left (*looking at Hazel*) not on the right but on the left and maybe some of you want to start making your way back there?

Tharwa *follows* **Tala** *to the back room.*

Tharwa   Is it OK if she?

Mason   Yeh, yeh.

Mason   You coming big man?

Hazel   No great you go Carl that'd be great.

Carl   Yeah.

Hazel   I'll go and check the room make sure it's OK.

Carl *turns upstage.*

Mason   Thanks.

Marc   Mum / eat now.

Beth   Yeah no yeah.

Mason   Cheers, Carl, that's great.

The sound of a bird lashing around.

Beth   What's that?

Mason   Oh Hazel said it was a bird / a bird that.

Beth   Fucking hell.

Mason   Yeh got trapped in the roof /

Beth   That's awful.

Mason   Can't find its way out.

Marc   Mum you gonna eat anything before it's cold or what?

Mason   We're going to start the choir in there so.

Marc   My mum needs to eat.

Beat.

Mason   No, I was thinking like, I was like, I your boy's a musician.

Beth   Fuck off.

Marc   MUM /

Mason   Right. OK yeh.

He begins to leave.

Beth   I'm sorry.

Fuck . . .

Enter **Hazel** *which stops* **Beth** *in her tracks.*

Hazel   OK . . .

Beth *eats. In the next room we begin to hear the sounds of the choir starting up. They need to be getting going to the court.*

Beth   Sorry like I was rude to that man.

She leaves.

Marc   Mum!

Beth *goes for a cigarette and* **Marc** *and* **Hazel** *are left alone for a minute.*

Hazel   What happened there?

Marc   Nothing she's just stressed and.

Beat.

Hazel   What time do you have to be at the court?

Marc   Oh yeh I . . . We're gonna be late.

She wanted to come see you like she's here now and you're like she's not talking.

Hazel   That's OK. Has she got everything? You OK?

Marc   Yeh. Got the papers they gave us /

Hazel   Phone bag yeh /

Marc   When they took her.

Hazel   We'll sort this all out.

Marc   Yeh. No of course. Sorry.

Marc   The food was really good.

Beat. He avoids, she notices.

Marc *stands up and faces the audience.*

The choir begins.

Hazel   And they're off.

Hazel   You OK, Marc?

Marc   Yeah I've told you.

Hazel   What time you gotta be at court?

Marc   Court starts at two but we have to be thirty mins early to meet the barrister.

Hazel   You got everything?

Marc   Yeah she has the papers from when she was taken.

Hazel   Don't get narky with me.

Pause.

Marc   Where is she?

Hazel   Is she coming back in or what?

Beth *re-enters.*

Beth   They had started / sorry.

Marc   We're gonna have to go soon Mum.

Beth   You got that three quid you said you had for dinner?

Marc   Yeh.

Marc *goes to the kitchen and makes a drink.*

Hazel   Listen remember you're gonna tell them, you're through with Jason.

Beth   I am through with him . . . Marc what are you doing?

Marc   Getting a drink.

Beth   What'll we have for dinner then, Marc? What do you think she'll want eh? Eh?

Marc   Chips probably.

Hazel   She likes chips.

Marc   They said she was too . . . skinny / she didn't weigh.

Beth   She's not.

Hazel   Your gonna get the bus yeah.

Cloud descends on **Beth**.

Beth   I'm gonna pee.

Hazel   You know you gotta arrive like fifteen minutes early to get through the metal detector and that? Can't have anything on you scissors or nail files.

Marc *looks through* **Beth** *'s bag, change in the music.* **Beth** *exits toilet.*

Beth   Marc plays guitar / you know.

Hazel   Oh wow.

Beth   He's my soulmate you know.

Hazel   You're gonna have to go.

Beth   And it's raining.

Fuck.

Beth *breaks down.*

Hazel   Hey hey.

Hey listen don't let them tell you about stuff from your stuff from before and blame you for nothing.

Beth   Just keep talking.

Hazel   You're a good mum.

Yeh? Focus on like the, love? The love in your heart. Right? You're a good mum.

Beth   Thanks, Hazel.

They can suck on my cunt.

Exit **Beth** *and* **Marc**.

Hazel *is tired, she begins to gather up the mugs, then there's a drop that falls from the roof. After a time,* **Bernard** *walks out of the room he is mumbling to himself.*

Hazel   You OK, Bernard?

Bernard   Yeh.

I just keep getting it wrong.

Hazel   Bernard . . .

Bernard   I can't sing and so I don't sometimes but the others are singing nicely around me so I can pretend that's me.

A time.

Hazel   Did you like the pasta?

Bernard   YEH.

Beat.

Proper Italian style.

Hazel   Really?

Bernard   I've been to Italy.

Hazel   Oh yeh.

What did you do there?

Bernard

Oh I was just walking around you know.

Walking around.

Talking to the people.

Living a bit like St Francis.

Beat.

Hazel   Oh OK. . .

How long was you there?

Bernard   Seven years.

Hazel   Right oh OK yeh.

Bernard   Yeh I was all fired up about things.

The drop falls.

Hazel   Oh God.

They look at it, simply.

Hazel   They came in here, the council, before Pete got sick /

Bernard   Oh /

Hazel   They're 'exploring options' for the place whatever that means /

Bernard   Oh /

Hazel   D'you want a biscuit? You didn't get a biscuit did you?

Bernard   No.

Maybe it'll stop raining anyway soon.

Hazel   You're a very beautiful person, Bernard.

Silence.

Mason *comes out very worried that* **Bernard** *isn't enjoying it?*

Mason   Are you coming back?

Is it OK?

Bernard   Yes yes I'm coming back alright.

Mason   Great.

Mason   Bernard's back.

They go back in, more singing, we can see them through the door.

Hazel *sits in silence, exhausted. Another drop falls.*

Blackout, very short.

Scene Two

Two hours later at most.

Lights up. The hatch is closed. The door to the outside area is open, we can see some light coming though, some voices off suggesting that the people that have been at the choir are just now leaving.

Hazel *is standing in a similar place . . Someone is smoking a rolled-up cigarette that we have noticed them rolling patiently and carefully in the previous scene in the* *courtyard-garden area.* **Anthony** *has been in the bathroom and is heading out. As he leaves he is held up by* **Bernard** . . .

Bernard *comes in.*

Hazel   Here's some food, I put some in for the little one too.

Tharwa   Thank you. The garden is nice.

Hazel   Oh yeh that's normally Pete, you'll meet him.

Tharwa   Thank you.

Tharwa *leaves.* **Bernard** *is sitting there.*

Enter **Mason** *with a bucket.*

Mason   Yeh I reckon that. . . / they'd better fix that.

Hazel   Yeh well Pete said that's gonna be really expensive . . . and they're not paying for it right now I mean the council.

Mason   Oh right . . .

I mean we could just get like a Kickstarter or a GoFund it page,

Silence.

Hazel   Really?

Mason   Yeh yeh yeh.

I mean people out there people out there they can just give?

Mason   I'll get my bag then / and that unless there's something that.

Hazel   OK / no no thank you, Mason.

Mason *goes to the kitchen area. He doesn't want to leave.*

Hazel (*to* **Carl** *sat alone*)   Carl where's your carer she late again?

Marc *enters.*

Carl   Um yeah.

Hazel   OK let's go look.

Carl   OK.

Hazel   How was the choir?

Carl   It was good.

Hazel   Good.

Hazel *sees* **Marc** *as they're walking towards the door.*

Mason   Alright man.

Hazel   Oh, Marc /

Marc   Mum's waiting outside.

Hazel   OK.

Marc   She like . . . Can you go speak / to her?

Hazel   OK.

Marc   She doesn't want to come in yet.

Hazel   Yeah OK. Give me one minute, Carl.

Mason   Shall I lock up, Hazel?

As she leaves 'Yes Please'. **Carl** *and* **Marc** *are left alone not knowing where to go they hover.*

Marc   . . . Sorry . . .

Carl *smiles at him, slowly peels off to a seat in audience.* **Marc** *alone.*

Marc   Sorry.

Mason   I'm just gonna lock up and that. Lock up.

Mason *is closing the door, struggling with it, making up reasons to be there.*

Bernard   Just push it before you pull it.

Mason   Cheers, mate.

Silence they all smile supportively at **Marc**. **Bernard** *then starts saying the lyrics to the tune.*

Bernard *hums the tune – or sings it because he CAN sing now he's on his own?*

Mason   Yeh that's it, Bernard.

We had the choir.

You into your music – your mum I heard – you're a musician.

Marc   I mean.

Yeh.

Basically I played / a bit and guitar? in my past yeh.

Mason   So you're a musician. /

Marc   I used to write songs and stuff.

Mason   We should definitely have a jam.

Marc   Cool no yeh collab definitely.

Mason   Definitely / yeh.

Marc   Cool.

Silence, **Marc** *looks towards the door.*

Mason   I know yeh your mum and that.

Marc   Yeh.

Mason   Hazel yeh I should /

He tries to leave.

Marc   Court and that the, I'm just gonna go and check on my mum.

Mason   It's cool mate I'll go get her it's ok.

Marc   No it's /

Mason   No you have a moment yeh chill. Stay here. I'll go.

Mason *maybe exits, doing too much, where he's not wanted or needed, he's made it worse.*

Marc *and* **Bernard** *are left for a moment –* **Bernard** *looks at* **Marc**.

Bernard   It's really annoying I can sing it in my head / but not aloud, or not so easily.

Marc   What the fuck.

Bernard   You know the song 'Three Little Birds'.

Bernard   Well sometimes it's quite nice to just hear it in your head play it in your head.

They do.

Marc   Yeh.

Enter **Hazel** *and* **Beth**, **Mason** *is obviously behind them, or there are sounds of him locking up.*

Hazel   I've just got a couple of things to do then we can go yeh together.

Beth   Thanks, Hazel.

Hazel   OK Bernard we're locking up.

Bernard   I'll go then.

Hazel   See you soon Bernard.

Bernard   I'm going then?

Hazel   OK yeh I've got to get to work don't I?

Hazel *is trying to get out of the door herself.*

Bernard   I'll be back here for coffee morning on Friday.

Hazel   Sure of course.

Bernard   OK.

Have a good Thursday.

Beat.

Bye.

Thank you.

Sorry.

Exits.

Beth *is in the corner somehow.*

Marc   Mum.

Beth   Yep.

I'm just gonna get some water.

She goes behind the screen now, her phone rings, she answers and then hangs up.
Marc *notices.*

Marc   Did she tell you?

Hazel   No she just said they / were horrible.

Marc   Mum.

Mum.

Beth (*from behind the screen*)   I'm coming.

She's back, wiping her mouth, she drank from the tap and has spilled loads of it on her.

Hazel   What happened?

Beth   Fuck them she went out of the house alone / for five minutes and they sent in the Nazis.

Marc   MUM let me explain you explain it then tell Hazel what the fuck happened Mum. / that wasn't it.

Hazel   Calm down yeh. OK tell me, Beth.

Beth   There was loads of them lawyers and fuck and they just said all this stuff I can't I can't remember you didn't fucking / say anything.

Marc   Mum fucksakes.

Hazel   Just calm down and tell me what happened /

Marc   They're going to start a load of investigations analysing and psychological reports mum has to get therapy and we need to find a guardian /and we've got twenty-six weeks to do it.

Beth   But / fuck . . . Marc?

Hazel A guardian.

Marc To help parent Faith but we /

Beth Fuck that they're just posh cunts they were bringing up my past and every person I fucked and everything about my life they had it all written . . . Hazel they want to take my kid they want to take my kid they were like you're a bad mother they said that! Marc / why didn't you speak more?

Marc They didn't say that, Mum /

Beth They fucking did why are you taking their side? Hazel . . .

YOU DON'T TRUST ME. YOU THINK IT'S MY FAULT? YOU AGREE why they were like you're broke and my past and they fucking . . . cunts CUNTS CUNTS FUCK.

If you'd been fucking watching her this / wouldn't have happened would it.

Hazel STOP . . . DO NOT TALK TO YOUR BOY LIKE THAT. We're gonna sort this out ok /

Marc You were asleep, Mum, yeh you were asleep that's the fucking issue isn't it Mum you were off your head on pills and asleep you fucked up.
Fuck you.

Beth WHAT THE FUCK DID YOU SAY / Hazel he's lying.

Marc (*shouting*) Fuck Mum I'm sixteen years old I'm sixteen you don't fucking put this on me you don't get to put this on me.

I was at college I had nothing to do with it.

Hazel STOP /

Beth Fuck this Marc you've left me /

Marc Sorry fuck sorry.

He goes to the kitchen.

Hazel What did you do that for?

Think, listen, yeh, listen.

Beth *looks at her, short pause.*

Beth They brought up everything how I was in care what happened in the home.

Hazel What.

Beth They even spoke about my mum.

Hazel.

Fuck.

Beth   Where is Faith? Where is my little girl? Where is she, Hazel?

Hazel   I don't know darling. I don't know. She's with the foster parents but she's OK now you need to listen to me.

Beth   I was just asleep for ten mins I left her and she wandered out on the road and was walking to the shops . . . ten minutes, Hazel. Fuck.

I'll call Jason I'll never / see.

Hazel   Good.

Beth   Him again.

They wouldn't do this if I had money, Hazel.

Hazel   I know love but /

Beth   Marc! Marc! I'm sorry Jesus Marc it's my fault Marc it's my fault I'm sorry.

Marc *and her hug, reconcile quickly they do this all the time – fight and make up, fight and make up.*

Beth   I'll do what they say. Hazel I'll ask for the therapy and.

I'll do.

Marc   We'll do.

Beth   We'll do whatever they want Hazel.

Beat.

Hazel   OK. OK let me think.

Who can you ask to help you parent her, to be the guardian while you do the things you need?

Beth   I . . .

I'll ask my aunt.

Hazel   But she's not . . . you told me you haven't spoken to her for years.

Beth   She's still my aunt.

Marc   Mum?

Beth   I'll ask her to be the guardian.

If I do what they say it's going to work isn't it Hazel it's going to work.

Short silence then in a soft voice:

Hazel   Yeh.

Yeh.

That'll work.

You better call Jason make sure he knows not to contact you. Call him now.

Marc can you just take those to the car please.

Beth *dials. Leaves a voicemail.*

Beth   Jason . . .

This is probably best as a voicemail, right, yeh.

You probably don't know this or want to hear this but I've decided.

It's best we don't speak and you need to make sure you do as we were told and you need to stay away.

Channelling the official tone of the lawyer.

This is final.

I'm ending this now then.

OK by/e.

Hazel   Block his number, call Gavin the social worker now yeah tell him you're gonna do what they ask aren't you.

Exit **Hazel**.

The bird in the roof makes a sound, **Beth** *is startled. She goes to call Gavin – enter* **Mason**, *unseen.*

She hangs up abruptly. Silence. She dials again.

PICK UP.

FUCK.

Hangs up. Worried. She gets up to not have to think.

Mason *is there.*

Beth   I'm sorry about before I tried to find you but you were doing the choir.

Mason   It's alright.

Beth   I didn't mean to be rude.

Mason   It's all good.

You OK?

She hugs him. Suddenly. It's strange, **Mason** *isn't comfortable. He gets her off him politely.*

Mason   OK yeh.

Yeh.

I was just checking if Hazel needed anything.

Beth   They've gone to her car.

Mason   OK.

Take care yeh.

Beat. He exits.

Now she sees **Carl** *who has been here all along, sitting in the audience, a witness.*

Beth   Is someone coming for you?

Carl   Soon.

I hope.

Blackout.

Act Two: Christmas

Six to eight weeks later. The community centre has moved into more insecure waters, and this is made clear by some marks in the walls that have become clear, some sense of damp encroaching onto the space. Two parts of the space have drops in them now as the roof has got worse.

There are Christmas decorations up and the tables have been laid out for a Christmas meal.

Anthony *is asleep in the corner. As the scene begins* **Tharwa** *enters. There is a sense of occasion, of it being Christmas, they are dressed appropriately.*

Bernard   Happy Christmas.

Carl   Yeh.

Enter **Mason** *with a bag of clothes, lays them out quickly.*

Bernard   We can sit.

Enter **Tharwa** *goes straight to the kitchen.*

Carl   I might go and wait outside.

Tharwa   Hello Hazel. Happy Christmas / I.

Hazel   Al Salama Alikim /   (*Arabic: Hello*)

Bernard   No it's cold cold you shouldn't /

Wait outside. (*To* **Carl**) Do you want a cup of tea?

Carl   OK.

Carl sits in audience, **Mason** *puts clothes out,* **Hazel** *comes out of the kitchen with tablecloths,* **Tharwa** *following* **Bernard** *to tea urn.*

Mason   A lot of warm ones in here isn't it.

Bernard   Four right?

Carl   Yeah.

Tharwa   Let me help you with that, Hazel, let me help you yes.

Tharwa *begins to set the table.*

Mason   I'll put these up a bit better and that.

Mason *goes to cross towards* **Tharwa** *makes a noise, it wakes* **Anthony**.

Anthony   Fuck sake.

Mason   Sorry.

Anthony   Sorry I.

Hazel   No no no love it's OK stay asleep.

Anthony   Sorry I . . .

Carl   Christmas is very traditional it's good /

Mason *has crossed to inspect* **Tharwa***'s table work.*

Mason   May/be.

Tharwa   It's OK.

Enter **Marc** *behind* **Tharwa** *exits to kitchen.*

Marc   Hey Mason /

Mason   Hello mate!

How are yah? Yeh.

Marc   All good yeh.

Mason   You wan/na.

Marc   Play yeh.

Hazel   Mason can you come and / help me with the.

Mason   I'll just get Marc set up there in the room yeh and.

Bernard   Happy Christmas.

Marc   Happy Christmas.

Enter **Beth** *as they leave.* **Bernard** *left alone in the space fixing the table cloth.* **Hazel** *notices* **Beth** *as she moves back to the kitchen.*

Hazel   Beth.

She steps forward.

Beth   Hi Hazel . . .

Hazel   Long time, let me just finish this up and we'll chat, good to see you.

Beth *has crossed over the stage.* **Anthony** *is mumbling to himself audibly and trying to get himself comfortable which is difficult with all the commotion.*

Anthony   These fucking people won't let me sleep what fuck.

Beth   What'd you say.

Anthony   Sorry.

Bernard   First sign of madness talking to yourself.

Anthony   What you saying / I'm not mad.

Bernard   I didn't say you were / mad.

Anthony   Fuck you / Bernard.

Tala   Mum.

Bernard   Very festive.

He turns away **Bernard** *keeps going* **Anthony** *gets up.*

Anthony   Alright Bernard (*goes outside*).

Bernard   Where are you going? Come back.

Sorry.

Tala *gets up and walks over to the puddle.*

Tala   Mum.

Beth   Hi Tala.

Beth   What are you doing?

Tala   There's a puddle.

Tala *and* **Beth** *jump in the puddle together.*

Tala   Mum.

Beth *hugs* **Tala**.

Tharwa *comes from the kitchen.*

Tharwa   Excuse me! What are you doing?

She takes her daughter from **Beth**.

Beth   SORRY lady I /

Tharwa   What are you doing get / off her get off her.

Beth   Sorry lady fuck.

They see that there's a drip and it's getting worse, **Bernard** *goes towards it.*

Bernard   We need a bucket.

Hazel *is coming out with the plates.*

Beth   This place is falling apart (*laughs.*)

Bernard   Happy Christmas.

Hazel *comes out with the petition and napkins.*

Hazel   Tharwa /

Tharwa   Yes.

Sorry.

Hazel   Can you sign my petition now, love?

Tharwa   What is it?

Hazel   Oh it's a petition.

There's an issue with the place and the council are meeting and that to . . . yeh about not selling this place.

Beth   I'll get Marc to sign it.

Beth *runs off, unnecessarily, as* **Marc** *already has.* **Tharwa** *might have wet hands or have her hands full.*

Hazel   You just need to sign your name and address.

Tharwa   You need my address?

Hazel   Yeah.

Tharwa   My hands are dirty I can't sign.

I sign it later.

Mason   Yeh Marcus would love this wouldn't he.

Carl *is visibly stressed.*

It's funny I spent last Christmas with Marcus he was going all crazy doing Christmas drawings / and shit.

Hazel   Yeh. /

Mason   Cos they won't even let you have decorations fucking / sorry.

Hazel   Yeh. Do you want to help me with the napkins?

Short silence, awkwardness hangs because Marcus has been mentioned.

Mason   I'm looking forward to seeing him what is it less than a month now isn't it till he's out?

Hazel   February.

Mason   Where's he gonna stay with you I guess or?

Hazel   .

Mason   Sorry I didn't mean to upset you.

Beat.

Hazel   I'm not upset.

You / alright, Carl?

Mason   / I thought you were then.

Carl   Yeh.

Mason   Yeh?

Hazel   Stop trying to read me. You'll know when I'm upset.

Mason   No no God.

It's all growth.

Hazel   Just finish the napkins /

Mason   Yeh I /

Mason *goes towards the kitchen after her,* **Bernard** *has been watching all of this throughout.*

Bernard   Mason can I have a word?

Mason *is trying to get to the kitchen.*

Mason   Yeh, Bernard.

Bernard   The choir's really good you know it's amazing the singing and all the stuff starts coming together and yeh I.

Mason   Oh cheers yeh thank you Bernard Happy Christmas and that to you.

Bernard   I think Christmas is a facist ceremony.

Enter **Beth**.

Beth   He's coming.

Carl   Can you get me a glass of water.

Mason   Look I've just gotta /

Bernard   I was wondering you know.

Beth   Yeh.

Mason   Yeh.

The below is very fast – there needs to be, musically, a feeling of text completely overlapping.

Bernard   I was wondering you know . . . I just can't help thinking all them people they all get a solo. I would like a solo you know I've been there since the very first rehearsal.

I just think it should be fair. Fairness is important.

Mason   No no Bernard mate totally. Just give me a minute yeh.

Bernard   Yeah.

Mason *goes to toilet,* **Anthony** *crosses and knocks.*

Bernard   There's someone in there.

Marc   Oh I didn't realise you were here?

Anthony   Here.

Marc   Yeah.

Anthony   That was really beautiful earlier.

Marc   Oh yeh? Cheers no . yeh . Just playing a bit with Mason.

Anthony   Yeh I. Just that you were great.

Tharwa *enters she's decided to do the petition. She has dirt on her hands but still decides to sign it.*

Tharwa   Hazel I have decided to sign the petition.

Carl   I want to sign it.

Hazel   No leave it for a minute yeh it's OK.

Carl   I will sign it. /

Anthony   It's alright, mate.

Carl   I want to sign it /

Hazel   It's ok, Carl I'll tell you about it later.

Mason *is back in.*

Carl   I don't want the place to close the library closed, Mason.

Marc   You wanna . . .

Mason   Sorry mate I gotta go to the kitchen.

Hazel   Yeh but it's fine don't worry yeh it's a procedure.

Anthony   It's not gonna clo/se.

Hazel   It's not gonna close there's like a process.

Carl *gets up to leave – he's suddenly quite upset at the situation and so walks out.* **Beth** *comes out of the toilet –* **Hazel** *emerges from kitchen and asks* **Mason** *to go into it.* **Tharwa** *is sitting with the petition, reading it.* **Mason** *goes into the kitchen, it's tense between them but* **Mason** *is trying to grow and reset relations.* **Beth** *catches* **Hazel** *on the way over to* **Carl**.

Beth   I meant to say I've brought some of Faith's clothes / in.

Hazel   What do you / mean?

Beth   Just she's outgrown them.

Hazel   It's been no / time.

Beth   They bought her some more.

Marc   Why you doing that you never said you'd / brought.

Hazel   Who.

Beth   Fuck – I don't know the foster family I think.

She's looked great.

I brought her her Wotsits the other time it was yeh.

I mean it doesn't help that Gavin's a cunt.

Laughs.

Hazel   What's he done.

They sit.

Beth   He made me late for the contact cos he keeps changing the place at the last minute.

Hazel   Oh no.

Tharwa   Hazel. Food is ready.

Hazel *tries to go but* **Beth** *stops her.*

Beth   Gavin keeps fucking calling.

Hazel   Hang on.

Marc   You've got to tell / her.

Bernard   I miss her.

Beth   I will I just need a / . . . drink.

Anthony   Who?

Bernard   Charity.

Short pause.

Hazel *goes to the kitchen.* **Marc** *looks at* **Anthony**, *embarassed but then exits. Beat* **Beth** *is in the kitchen and then goes to* **Carl** *out back.*

Anthony   Why d'you keep telling people things / even on Christmas?

Tharwa   Hazel the food is ready.

Anthony   I choose to remember Charity's life how I remember Charity's life yeh.

Hazel   Come and get some food.

She goes to go and get the food and serves it. It's a simple meal but it's still a Christmas meal.

Tharwa (*in Arabic*)   Come on it's time to eat now.

Outside, slowly, it begins to rain. **Carl** *comes in.*

Carl   It's fucking raining again.

Hazel   Carl.

Carl   It's really good the soup.

Mason   You've had it before haven't you mate.

Marc (*to* **Beth**)   Do you want some.

Beth   Yeh yeh.

Tala   Thank you.

Mason   Bread there if you want some.

Mason (*to* **Tharwa**)   Happy Xmas . . . sorry.

Hazel   When's she coming back your friend?

Anthony   Don't worry about it.

Anthony *sits at the table.*

Tala   I like your hat.

Anthony   Thanks Happy Christmas.

Tala   Happy Christmas to you too.

They eat.

Beth   It's really nice, Hazel.

Hazel   Thanks. It's my Christmas stew.

Bernard   It's delicious, better than last year.

Hazel   Oh Bernard.

Mason   Yeh it's really.

Hearty /

Anthony   It really is.

Mason   Yeh there's veg.

Anthony   Thank you, yeah.

Mason   Merry Christmas.

General thank yous, A round of applause.

Tharwa   Thank you Hazel!

Carl   It's delicious!

*A community member (***Irene***) goes to get salt.*

Tharwa (*in Arabic*)   Please eat what's in front of you.

Marc   Mum pass the bread.

*A community member (***Leigh***) goes to get water.*

Mason   Water.

Tharwa (*to* **Anthony**)   Do you study?

Anthony   At some point.

Beth *goes to get seconds.*

Marc (*to* **Beth**)   You getting more?

Hazel (*coming out of the kitchen*)   It's hot in there.

Tharwa (*in Arabic*)   Do you remember the cat we saw on the way here?

Tala *laughs.*

Mason   Does anyone else want some more?

Anthony *gets up to get more food. As he returns,* **Bernard** *coughs,* **Anthony** *spills some food.*

Anthony   Sorry sorry.

Tharwa   It's OK it's OK.

Carl *becomes increaseingly agitated.*

Marc   Carl you OK yeh.

Carl *crosses to the toilet.*

Mason   Is he alright?

Hazel   They cut his carer hours.

Anthony   Sorry Hazel yeah.

Hazel   Don't worry.

Tharwa (*in Arabic*)   Shall we give out the cake?

Marc *gets up to make a drink.*

Marc   Does anyone want a drink?

Tharwa   Yes please.

Mason   Marc was playing really well weren't you.

Beth   Yeah.

Marc   Yeh.

Carl *re-enters.*

Silence.

Carl   There's a . . . it's not right like they.

I don't like it I don't like it one day it's going to blow up in their face.

The powerful they'll blow up.

Mason   What, mate?

Beat.

Carl   But if we do the choir concert, Mason?

Mason   Yeh, Carl.

Carl   The concert the concert the concert will be good good I think /

Hazel   What concert.

Carl   I think yeh we should do the concert I do.

Mason   Actually yeh.

Bernard was yeh?

Talking about the choir earlier. I mean if it gets much worse there's gonna be an armed rebellion. I'm going to fight. Fuck that it'd be me and the person that's there with me . . . I'll be willing to fight. If it comes down to it I'm happy to use . . . resistance. I mean yeh things can't be like this much longer and I don't know about the vaccine or what's in it or if we're got the same one as them? D'you know what I mean my heart is pure but if it comes to it I mean anyway it's all good / so like sorry love?

Tala *brings around a little bit of cake in a box that they've prepared for the community centre.*

Tala   Do you want one we made it.

Mason   Oh thank you.

Generalised improvised expressions of happiness. Counterpoint to the situation.

Tala   Do you want one?

Bernard   Thank you. That's a very kind thing to do.

Hazel   Oh wow thank you.

Tharwa   We wanted to give you all some present to say thank you.

She hands it around to be improvised, improvised thank yous.

She the leaves it on the table and **Tharwa** *puts it back in the bag.*

Tharwa   Thank you.

Hazel   Sorry Anthony you didn't get much rest everyone'/ s.

Anthony   No it's OK.

Marc   Does anyone want a tea?

Mason (*to* **Beth**)   I mean.

I get it like the roof IS falling apart but that kind of structure needs attention and care and that /

Beth   Yeh.

No love.

Hazel   Thanks Mason /

Marc   Sorry does anyone want a tea?

Bernard   Yes thanks.

Mason   Sorry I /

Hazel   No it's OK..

No love, actually yeh.

Mason   Yeh . . . no yeh.

Carl   If we if we . . . do the concert then maybe that'd be good?

Hazel   Well we'll start with the petition and that and see won't we and Pete will be back. . . .

Bernard   Pete's in hospital. I tried to go see him.

Hazel   Did you?

Bernard   He's . . .

Short silence.

Hazel   Yeah. He's OK. But like your crowd funding is going alright.

Mason   Yeh.

Beat. It's not.

Carl *is a bit disappointed.*

Mason   Yeh I mean it's going alright yeh /

There's a drop. they eat. Silence, people are finishing. **Tharwa** *has a couple of beats in Arabic.*

Bernard   I'm going to shave.

He exits to the bathroom.

Hazel   That cake was delicious.

Tharwa   Thank you. We are going to go. Hazel.

Hazel   Thank you for your help today.

She hesitates. Hugs her and leaves.

Tharwa   Tala.

Tala   Bye.

Beth   Bye!

Short silence – someone gets up and goes for a cigarette. **Hazel** *looks at the drop.*

Beth *looks at* **Marc**.

Beth   Let me show you the video, Hazel.

Marc   MUM.

Beth   Let me show you the video of her today.

Marc you've got your guitar, go and.

Her phone rings.

Hazel   You / gonna.

Marc   Mum no /

He goes.

Hazel   Have you spoken to your aunt though / about being the guardian.

Beth *is in denial.*

Beth   I have yeh.

I mean it's a mess isn't it like.

We got her all her favourite food and I made her a special t-shirt I coloured it in myself.

She shows the photo.

Mason   NICE!

Beth   I drew all the letters of her name in a different colour 'F A I T H' and made them all look different like F is a trumpet A is like two people leaning into each other I is like a really thin snake T is a tree and H is . . . I don't know I couldn't think of anything for H! So it's just an H.

Hazel   That's so nice.

Beth   Yeh and she really loved it she was like MUM!!!!

Mason   / Amazing.

She opens the file.

Beth   He'll be back.

Hazel   It's OK love.

Calls out.

Beth   Marc!!!

Hazel *clears the bowls.*

Hazel   Did you speak to her though?

Beth *deflects with the video.*

Beth   LOOK OK look.

Beth *plays the video out of her phone.*

Beth   Marc wrote this song for her.

Beth *and* **Hazel** *stand over* **Beth***'s phone watching a video of* **Marc** *playing something to Faith on his guitar and you can hear Faith laughing and enjoying the song.* **Mason** *stands apart but is listening and trying to watch too. There is a long pause once the video ends. There is nothing to say.*

Eventually **Hazel** *walks back to the kitchen, where she stumbles and falls – we don't see the fall but there is a loud crash as she has fallen into plates and pots and pans. Everyone comes running to help* **Hazel***.*

Hazel   I'm sorry.

Sorry yeh it's all good.

Sorry.

I'm fine I'm fine.

Mason   Oh Jesus sorry.

Hazel   Everything is fine don't worry about me I just lost my footing for a minute.

Hazel   I'm fine it's nothing, honestly it's all good.

I'll just.

Beth   Do you want me to come with you?

Hazel   I just lost my footing.

I'LL JUST.

Let me get some air for a minute.

Beth   OK.

A pause.

Anthony   Hazel?

Hazel   Leave me for a second yeh. Anthony!

Anthony *goes out.*

Mason   You gotta come to the choir and h/ear Marc.

Beth   I might yeh I might go and see if (*Hazel*)

Mason   I'd leave her she'll be back in a minute.

He sings a few lines to her humming from the music that is offstage.

She sings back for a bit.

Sorry I just.

Beth   No.

Mason   I felt like singing.

She sings back for a bit.

Beat. What is happening . . . danger. **Anthony** *goes to knock on the toilet door.*

Mason   There's another one out back by the exit.

Anthony   Yeh . . .

He goes.

Beth   .

Mason   But yeh you should come to the choir / it's a family atmosphere.

Beth   Oh I /

Mason   I mean.

Beth   Yeh?

Mason   You should it'd be great and that / and.

Beth   Yeh. Sorry I'm just what with the.

Mason   Of course I mean I get it.

Mason   I know this sounds weird but did we know each other when we were . . . Younger did you grow up in Scotland? Like.

Beth   No but then I yeh I moved here as a kid when my mum . . .

Mason   So weird I just like I dunno I keep doing that like I meet people and I'm like 'I've seen you before' (*laughs*) it's proper weird like.

Mason   When I was a kid right.

Beth   Yeh.

Mason   Yeh so I anyway.

I just had this group of friends and we'd do mad shit and you looked like.

Beth   Yeh? Oh cool.

Re-enter **Hazel**.

Mason   Yeh you looked like someone I knew but I mean fuck.

Anyway it's all good sorry I didn't, Hazel you OK?

Hazel   I'm just gonna do some stuff in the kitchen.

Mason   No yeh totally.

Beth *'s phone rings again.*

Beth   I've gotta to answer this.

Mason   No.

Yeh go ahead.

Carl   Hazel do you need help?

Hazel   Yeh OK come in yeh.

*A community member (**Leigh**) enters in from the garden, they have been drinking a beer.*

Mason   Sorry love you can't drink in here.

*Short silence, **Beth** comes in she's about to go to **Hazel** but she is stopped by him for a moment.*

Mason   I'm sorry about Faith.

Beth   No that's OK.

Mason   I mean they're cunts (*laughs.*)

Beth   I've done everything.

Hesitates.

I mean I'm happy to DO therapy but there isn't any like I asked the doctor he was like it's a year's wait to get therapy. So that's fine but what you meant to do for that time just hope you don't kill yourself? Anyway you'd love my daughter you should meet her she'd like you she's musical too.

Mason   Oh yeh?

Anthony *knocks on the door.*

A noise from inside, he steps away.

Anthony   FUCKSAKES.

Mason   There's another bathroom behind the stairs.

Anthony   Yeh but the light's not working in that one.

Mason   It is I.

Anthony   OK thank you.

Beth   Yeh so anyway.

Sorry like I just.

No it's just it's hard to find people to talk to isn't it. / It's.

Mason   Of cou/ rse.

Beth   I'm just, yeh? Yeh I'm saying, it's hard to have a fucking conversation with someone / that's like.

Mason   Yeh like / agreeing and understanding / no.

Beth   No / yeh / about something actually. That happened to you and / no-one.

Mason   Right /

Mason   No when I was a kid it was the opposite they would turn a blind eye to people shouting in the house or whatever it was just normal.

Beth   Yeh some of the things Jason / says you'd not believe.

Marc   Mum /

Bernard   Anthony you know, you should knock gently, because of the the mirror.

Anthony   What about it?

Bernard   I can't see in the other one.

And my HAND TREMBLES / so when people come in I need a great deal of concentration in order to shave safely.

Mason   OK lads.

Bernard   EVERYONE has a right to safety.

Anthony   Man you can't just do what you want and expect everyone else to just fit in /

Bernard   I don't want you banging on the door like that when I'm shaving. I'm not safe. I'm not safe.

Mason   OK man.

Anthony   I didn't bang on the door.

Bernard   You banged on the door.

I HEARD YOU BANGING. I FELT IT.

Anthony   I didn't bang on the door.

*Enter **Beth** and **Hazel**; the following line is very public:*

Why is he accusing me of something I've not done? Why is he?

Hazel   Bernard leave it.

Bernard   I come to this place to be in peace / not to be.

Anthony   Everyone has a right to use the bathroom.

He storms into the toilet.

Hazel   There's some pudding for Christmas anyone wants any.

The pudding is served at the hatch.

Beat.

Marc   It's really nice, Hazel.

Beth   Yeh really good thank you thank you, Hazel.

Hazel   Tesco they donated it.

Beth   Yeh but you've cooked it a special way.

Hazel   No but thanks /

Silence people eat.

Carl   I always loved custard, Hazel.

It reminds me of school.

Bernard   Me too in fact yeh / at school I used to.

Mason   It's great that / sorry Bernard?

Bernard   No . . no . . .

Hazel   Enjoy.

Bernard   Thank you it's delicious.

Hazel   Oh Bernard you always know what to say.

Silence, they look at the drip.

Bernard   The developers will buy it and turn it into flats.

Mason   I guess they.

Yeh.

Beth *gives* **Marc** *a hat from the bag she has got from the pile.*

Anthony *is sitting in another chair maybe in the audience.*

Bernard   The developers will buy it.

Anthony   I thought your singing was well nice I heard it earlier and.

Marc   Cheers /

Anthony   No / just.

Marc   Cheers /

Anthony   Yeh no it's cool.

Beat.

Bernard   There's a building down there called the 'Riviera Lair'. . .

It doesn't look like a Riviera Lair to me . . . there's a problem with people how they are living. / They just don't have a 'relationship' to where they're living anymore.

Mason   That's just the names they give them.

Hazel   OK yeh but the cro/wdfunding and that.

Bernard   In some places thes/e relationships do exist. I mean if you plant a tree and you've been the one that's planted it /

Mason   No, Bernard /

Anthony   What tree, Bernard, there aren't any trees here /

Bernard   All I'm saying . . . when I was younger. There was a time when I was convinced of things that then turned out to not be so true, after all. It was a disappointment to me. I'd have been better off not trying so hard to fit in.

Hazel   Alright, Bernard? Sorry . . .

Bernard   People'd leave you alone then . . . anyone who is fitting in is already a fucking psychopath / Anthony. A fucking psy cho path.

Hazel   Alright Bernard don't worry.

Mason   There's no way they're gonna sell it.

Anthony   Fuck man.

Hazel   Yeh they're just saying that aren't they but once I get that petition and that.

Marc   OK.

Mason   Yeh once you've got the petition and that and they can.

Recognize. Yeh? Recognize that it's a 'public utility' that it's a community building people will be against them selling it and they won't be able to.

Marc   You staying?

Anthony   Yeh for a bit.

Mason   And they have to get approval right.

Hazel   Yeh yeh.

Bernard   I used to walk at night in this abandoned industrial estate near where I lived. Once found a pond in one and went swimming in it with a girl. (*Laughs.*)

Hazel   / They've spoken about this before two years ago.

Mason   Yeh yeh.

Hazel   They said it's not full market value and stuff cos it's empty yeah.

Carl   I saw this thing on TV where they did a lot of work to a house they rebuilt it actually.

Mason   Oh yeh I know the kind of programme you mean.

Carl   It was a glass house actually it was amazing you could see into it but it didn't rain in it and it was really woo hoo! Thank God for that. Did you see it, Hazel?

Hazel   No.

Carl   Don't you like TV?

Hazel   Yeh I like to watch TV.

But only a bit I only watch them nature /

Mason   Oh yeh nature programmes David / Attenborough.

Bernard   I know the ones you mean.

Hazel   Attenborough.

Blue Planet yeh.

Carl   Oh yeh.

Hazel   Yeh there's all of life in there.

Beat, motherly.

The other day I was watching about the salmon.

Do you know about the salmon?

People listen to her here.

It lays its eggs and then it dies, the female salmon. . . . but he sits there with her the salmon and waits till she gets over the drama of dying and that and then he swims off with the eggs.

But he sits there with her takes care of her.

When I saw that I was like, OH . . .

Mason   Oh right yeh.

He waits for her to die.

Then does he? He keeps going does he?

Hazel   Yeh he just swims off but he stays with her right it's kind of like that and the meercats?

Carl   Yeh.

Hazel   They are just like humans the same.

It's all there the animals take care of each other.

Cycle of life /

Carl   / cycle of life. Yeh.

Silence.

Bernard   That makes me want to sing /

Mason   Maybe actually it'd be a nice idea to I mean maybe we should do that concert that, Bernard?

Bernard   Oh, right.

Marc   Does anyone want tea?

Hazel   Yeh.

Mason   That it'd be good to do a concert I was thinking maybe obviously it'd have been better to do it for Christmas but that's going to be hard I think so (*laughs*) but you know fuck it we could so easily go and do it maybe even sing and go and sing outside the council offices and that why not you know raise awareness.

Carl   Raise awareness.

Hazel   No, Mason. (*She's smiling though.*)

Bernard   I'd like to be part of it. But the developer will still buy it.

Hazel   I don't know about / that but if it will help.

Anthony   Maybe you're right the developer will buy it and it'll be expensive flats and that but you can't just say things like that like that and yeh make people / despair.

Bernard   Despair down by the Riviera Lair.

Hazel   OK . . .

Anthony   All them people I've known these last years not one of them has come and put out an arm to me and that like you have Hazel /

Bernard   I'm not saying that if this or places like this are stopped / it'd be a good thing for anyone or.

Anthony   So if no arm is outstretched you / fall into the end.

Hazel   OK just eat your cake yeh,

Anthony   Sorry, Hazel sorry,

Bernard   Sorry . . .

Small beat.

Anthony   You don't know everyone's shit and what is fair /

Bernard   THERE IS NO FAIRNESS.

Anthony   Sorry mate. Fuck. Fuck this guy. Life man!

Marc   Alright.

Bernard   You've always got it in for me.

I WILL NOT BE BULLIED.

No no no no no.

I will not be bullied.

AH!!!!!

Mason   Alright, Bernard, it's all good, it's all good yeh?

Yeh?

Anthony   You don't know what it is, all you do is SHOUT SHOUT.

Because when someone saying something you don't like you can do is shout /

(*Community member (* **Leigh***) goes to the garden to drink, another community member (* **Irene***) leaves*)

Bernard   I'M NOT SHOUTING.

Anthony   You SHOUT at your age, I shout my age. Everyone is allowed to shout at whatever age they are, BERNARD where I'm from / if you shout.

Bernard   I am not saying that the world is not fucked up I'm not saying that it's not / fucked up.

Anthony   YOU don't know you / don't know.

Bernard   WILL YOU LISTEN TO ME /

Anthony   BERNARD.

Hazel   Calm down, Anthony.

Anthony   But hear me now when you talk about this country you need to know in some places you walk on the street and it isn't words it's weapons that speak, the only thing people hold onto is an ending.

BAMAMAMAAB.

BAMAMAMAAB.

BAMAMAMAAB aghh!!!!!!!

LISTEN TO ME, BERNARD you don't like guns I don't like them either.

Hazel   Calm down Anthony or you're gonna have to leave.

Bernard   Anthony /

Anthony   But you're not listening to me, Bernard, yeh.

Begging.

Feel the rage of my youth, yeh, feel the rage of my youth, Bernard.

If you're alive! You're alive . . . And that's good yeh / yeh.

Bernard   I know there's worse I know in this country I'm not saying that.

Anthony   There's always someone worse. What you will follow you will follow and what I will follow I will follow. But that's not to say . . . my friend Charity. FUCK.

There's ghosts everywhere, Bernard. Everywhere.

Beat.

Bernard   Anthony . . . I'm not saying I'm superior to you.

Anthony   No . . .

Anthony   You're not / superior.

Marc   Just leave it . . .

Bernard (*fast, as if he finally has space to speak his creed*)   For me it's a person is a person, it's what they are, it's what they have in them.

Anthony   Right, right in their guts /

Bernard   And what a person is, a person it's hard but it's hard but what we have to admit that we are not the best. But we are not the worst either are we.

Anthony   No, yeh. / No.

Bernard   We are not the worst but we are not the best either.

Mason   Yeh.

They sit for a while.

Mason   Bernard I deliberately haven't given you a solo because I thought. . . / AGH. You know?

Anthony   Bernard I'm sorry.

Bernard   It's OK, Anthony . . . I'm it's OK . . .

Mason   Let's see about that concert eh?

Short silence.

Bernard   Sorry.

Anthony   I'm sorry.

Marc   It's OK.

Mason   I'll.

To the community member (**Leigh***) who has just re-entered and taken a coat.*

Did you want a bag for that or?

Leigh   Yep.

Bernards *got up.*

Bernard   I'm sorry I'm going to leave.

Hazel   No, Berna . . .

He's walked out.

Anthony   I'm gonna go and have a cigarette.

Hazel   There's more if you want.

Silence. No-one goes to take more. After a time, **Hazel** *gets up a bit defeated.*

Hazel   OK . .

We'd better start to yeh, if you can give us a hand.

Beth *is a bit in retreat, . . . she looks at* **Marc**.

Marc *looks at her, Maybe says 'Mum' under his breath. They need to tell* **Hazel**.

She jumps up.

Beth   Yeh.

Mason   Chairs, Marc yeh /

Marc   Where?

Beth   Where do you want these. . . .

Hazel?

Hazel   Sorry love yeh just put them up there on the counter /

Carl *is the centre of the stage and slowly holding the attention of the audience. He is slowly folding the tablecloth, methodically. This is what is telling the story.*

Hazel   Carl?

Carl   The tablecloth. The tablecloth, Hazel.

Hazel   Oh just here love.

She takes them.

Thank you. You OK, Carl?

Carl   Yeh.

Hazel   Do you want the Matchsticks, Carl?

Carl   Yeh. I didn't get one. Thank you /

Mason   Just push the legs in.

Carl   It would be good to have a concert, yes, I think Hazel?

Hazel   I suppose it could / be yeh I don't know.

Oh I don't know if you think it's a good idea Carl.

Carl   I want to do it.

To raise awareness.

Mason   I'm just gonna head off.

Hazel   Ok thanks Mason.

Marc   Bye Hazel.

Mason *leaves.* **Marc** *is hanging back, walks out.* **Carl** *heads to the bathroom.* **Hazel** *and* **Beth** *are left alone. There is a feeling of defeat.*

Hazel   Maybe they will do that concert, that'd be a good idea wouldn't it maybe to do it?

We're gonna sort this out.

By now there's just **Hazel** *alone, on stage.* **Beth** *almost sneaks up behind her.*

Beth   Yeh, Hazel?

Hazel *doesn't hear her at first. In this moment it's really important that there is a kind of mystery.*

Hazel *wanders over to the pictures on the wall, straightens them.* **Beth** *is lingering behind.*

Beth   My aunt.

She said she wouldn't do it.

Looks at her.

She said she wouldn't take Faith.

Hazel   What?

When?

Beth   Last week.

Hazel   Why?

Beth   I haven't seen her for years.

Hazel   Why didn't you tell me?

Beth   I wanted to. Mason was being nice to me and I just . . .

They're gonna take her . . . Hazel.

Hazel   What.

Beth   They're gonna take Faith. They told me they're doing like a . . . mental assessment and they've decided . . .

Silence.

Beth   Hazel (*she looks away*)

Hazel   I mean.

I can do it.

We're gonna sort this.

Not just leave it you know.

Beth   You'd do that.

Really?

Hazel   Yeh we can speak to Gavin the social worker what's his name.

Yeh I'm just not gonna let it be like that.

They can't just take her from you.

Just till you get things sorted I'll do it I'll be the guardian.

I'll take care of her.

I'm not having it, no.

Beth You'd have to say though that you'd do it till she's eighteen though and.

Hazel Yeh I know that I'd just.

Yeh look let's call Gavin.

Beth *hugs her.*

Beth I need to tell Marc.

Hazel Tell him to get that concert going yeh.

Tell him . .

She's alone on stage.

Immediately regrets her decision. Goes after **Beth** *but* **Carl** *comes out of the toilet. They look at each other.*

Blackout.

Act Three: Valentine's Day

Ten weeks later. The beginning of February. It is the coldest week of the year and they wear corresponding layers.

There has obviously been flooding inside the building. Puddles of water, drips, and the light in the kitchen is flickering.

Mason *comes in with a few things from the back room, followed by* **Hazel**.

Mason   These are less damaged like.

Hazel   OK we can't let anybody go in there now if they.

Mason   No no out of bounds.

Hazel   If there was an accident or what /

Mason   Totally get it.

Hazel   Oh Mason what about the piano?

Mason   Fuck.

He runs into the other room to go and get the piano.

Hazel   Does it still work?

Mason   Let's see. Get me a cloth.

Hazel *looks out the window.*

Moment of suspense. **Mason** *turns it on.*

Mason   OK.

It doesn't work at first, silence.

In silence he realises it's probably broken.

Hazel   Is it broken?

Can you get another one?

Mason   Not likely.

I should have.

Taken it home with me.

It's been really bad in there the last couple of weeks this rain is freakish like fair enough I've never seen it that before it's so foul like the roof and Marc hasn't been using it for ages so I could've just taken it home it's worse than last year fucking freakish storm shit. Sorry. Sorry Hazel.

Ah . . .

He's really upset but he tries again, nudges the keyboard around in some way.

He presses a button and one of the preset Musacks comes on.

Oh thank God thank God!

Hazel   Amen.

They laugh.

Mason   We'll do the choir practice in here right?

Hazel   Yeh.

Hazel *sits and thinks about the lunch.*

Enter **Tharwa** *with* **Tala**.

Tharwa   Hi Hazel what happened here today?

Hazel   Yeh oh I'm so sorry.

We aren't able to do a lunch today, we've had some flooding and the kitchen is out /
and Mason.

Mason   We've had /

Hazel   And I, we've had to fix it / yeh.

Mason   Fix it yeh sorry so / sorry.

Hazel   Sorry about the lunch I put it on my facebook /

Tharwa   Oh so there is no food?

Tala (*to* **Mason**)   Is there still the choir??!

Mason   Oh yeh.

Yeh we'll do it but it's gonna be down here that's all.

Tharwa (*in Arabic*)   Tala come to me.

Tala   But we'll miss the choir.

Tharwa (*in Arabic*)   We come back for the choir.

Hazel   I'm so sorry.

Tharwa   No.

It's OK it's OK.

Tala   I'm hungry.

They go to the shops.

Hazel   But we have biscuits and.

Tharwa   No no it's OK thank you.

Thank you.

Tala   Bye, Hazel.

Tharwa   OK.

Hazel   Sorry.

They leave, Silence.

We must have something something we can.

She goes to the kitchen opens the hatch for a bit – we see some damage through it.

Maybe some sandwiches? I've got bread.

Mason   There's cheese.

Silence. Long silence as they make food in silence – they are rebuilding something.

The bird flutters, they don't speak about it.

Gently, there are a few lines about how to cut the sandwiches – **Mason** *is cutting everything like for children, in fours.* **Hazel** *notices.*

Hazel   Cut it like this, like adult?

Mason   Yep of course OK.

Silence again.

This is alright this is.

Smiles, he's filled with joy.

I remember when I was growing up we used to go off for like ages in the woods and like sit there and look after ourselves and yeh and have sandwiches. That was alright that was. But and the staff they didn't like it and they'd get bare angry and that.

Hazel   How old were you?

Mason   Oh twelve.

Yeh.

But do you get that? Like for me my brain there are just bits about my childhood it goes blank like a CD you know that's scratched it just skips around and yeh I just can't remember bits.

He takes a bite of sandwich, then, with his mouth full, responding.

Hazel   You don't need to . . .

Mason   The? /

Hazel   Yeh tell people yeh about the sale or that / I.

Mason   No no.

Silence.

Did they say when we have to leave?

Hazel   I mean I'm waiting to hear they're meant to call me so they'll do that any day now yeh . . . Like if it's gone through or not.

The sale.

Cos if it hasn't then we could stay here indefinitely actually like people stay in places even if technically they are sold.

Anyway.

She looks at her phone which is sitting on the table next to them alongside her keys or something.

They'll call if they need to won't they?

Beat. **Bernard** *comes out from the backrooms.* **Mason** *notices him.*

Mason   You OK, Bernard?

Hazel   Hi Bernard.

Bernard   I just was yeh I was there.

I'm really looking forward to the choir.

Mason   Oh all good mate yeh.

Silence. **Bernard** *gets what's going on.*

Bernard   We're doing the choir though?

Hazel   Yes Bernard don't you worry we're doing the choir.

Bernard *wanders over to the window, to* **Mason**.

Mason   We just have to do it in here.

Hazel   Alright love do you want to sit over there?

It's still a bit early.

Enter **Marc** *who lurks about; they don't notice him at first.*

Hazel *looks at* **Bernard**, *the flooding has upset her.*

Hazel   Bit of a shock with what the piano and yeh.

Bernard   Yes . .

Hazel   We thought it was broken.

Beat, **Bernard** *hears a joke in his head before saying it.*

Bernard   Well singing clears the cobwebs right away.

Hazel   Marc what you doing here?

Marc   Are you open yeh?

Hazel   Yes sorry we've had flooding Marc sorry /

Marc   Cool. Have you seen my mum is she here like / sorry I thought maybe she'd come here that's all so yeh.

Hazel   No . .

Marc   It's all good just.

If you see her can you tell her to turn her phone on? Or call me she's been engaged for like an hour.

Mason   Yeh.

Sure thing mate we'll tell her.

Marc   Cheers thanks yeh.

Mason   Do you want a sandwich.

Marc   Yeh sorry I just thought she might be here and that so.

Marc *exits. A beat.*

Mason   I might just go and check if he / needs anything help or whatever he's not been.

Hazel   Yeh.

Mason   I'll be quick yeh.

Beat. **Hazel** *and* **Bernard** *are left here.*

Hazel   You tired yeh?

Bernard   No no sorry I'll check on Pete's plants.

Beat.

Hazel   I was looking forward to doing the chicken today and.

I got all sorts of things for it.

Bernard   Yeh.

I like chicken you're a good cook.

Silence, rain.

Bernard *wanders to the window and sees there's a mayfly there.*

Bernard   Oh watch it a bit for a second – yeh – just wait a second it's a mayfly.

They shouldn't be born now! It's the wrong time of year it shouldn't be here yet . . You only see them near trees normally in town and there aren't that many of them it must be lost . . and it's born at the wrong time of year . . . what is it.

Hazel   It's Valentine's Day.

Bernard   Poor bastard only lives a day and he's lost. And it's raining.

That's bad luck.

Hazel   He's all alone there is he?

He nods to his bags, as she's allowed him to sleep here tacitly, no-one else knows.

Bernard   Yeah.

Beat. **Carl** *knocks on the window.*

Erm.

Thank you Hazel.

Enter **Carl**.

Hazel   Hi Carl.

Carl   Hi Hazel.

It's pretty wet out there.

Hazel   Yeh.

Carl   That's bad, fuck!

Hazel   Woh.

We've had flooding in her / e.

Carl   Oh no. Is there still food?

Hazel   Yeh they're sandwiches sorry about the hot lunch.

We're gonna have to move you today as well because we've had to put the piano there today OK? I.

Carl   That's different.

Hazel   You want a sandwich?

Carl   I'll wait.

She sits **Carl** *in a different position, that of the front row – so he's watching the action with the audience.*

Laughs.

Hazel   You OK?

Carl   It's different.

Hazel   I know sorry.

Hazel *brings him a sandwich.*

Carl   Do you you want any help?

Are people coming?

Hazel   I don't know I put it on my facebook and that about the flooding but people will still come for the choir we're gonna do the choir.

Carl   OK.

Thank you.

Enter **Mason** *and* **Marc**.

Hazel   Oh you're wet.

Marc   It's raining again.

Beat.

Hazel   Did you find her?

Mason   No but she's read the Whatsapp that Marc sent her.

Hazel   What happened . . . What happened?

Marc   Nothing really it was going OK at the birthday contact and that but then so yeh my mum saw that there was CCTV cameras in the contact centre and shit.

Hazel   What /

Marc   Yeh they were recording the meeting so my mum said if you're gonna record me I'm gonna record you and she got her phone out and started filming the social workers.

He's sort of proud of her and clicks his fingers.

Mason   Fuck.

Marc   Anyway Gavin was like we're terminating the contact so my mum swore and they were like it's finished and mum went off.

Hazel   OK so she left before speaking to Gavin? Right.

Just gonna go check the car, see if I locked it properly.

Beat, she walks off.

Marc   Yeh.

Beat.

Thanks yeh for coming and that again.

Mason   S'alright mate.

Marc   I mean sorry it was really cool of you to let me come and play here and stuff.

Mason   Mate it was great to work with you.

Mason *wanders over to the keys, plays a few notes.* **Marc**'s *wandering off.*

Mason   You OK Marc yeh?

Marc   Yeh no cheers I mean they won't leave my mum alone it wasn't her fault at all? She's trying, she's got some hours at Tesco.

Mason   No fair enough I get that.

Short pause.

Marc   But so like I was at college . . . and that and Jason had just left . . .

Mason   Yeh /

Marc   And mum was really upset . . . so she'd taken a sleeping tablet and was in bed and we had the delay in the fucking universal credit, we just had no money. When we're hungry we just go to sleep.

Enter **Hazel** *unseen by* **Marc**.

Mason   Right.

Marc   I should have told the judge that . . . she was walking that morning down the main road from our house, towards Jason's and the cars . . .

She's only four . . . she wanted everyone to be happy.

Mason   Marc was just sharing . . . he's been very brave . . . go on mate.

Anthony *enters looks at* **Marc**.

Anthony   Hey Marc?

Marc   Sorry.

He goes to the loo.

Anthony   Y'alright Hazel?

Haze   Yea.

Hazel   I'm sorry love there's no hot food today we had flooding and . . . /

Anthony   No I get it I saw the post . . . I just don't know if you needed any help or.

Hazel   No it's OK we /

Anthony   Ok cool yeh no it's OK Hazel.

He sits.

Anthony   You here for the choir Carl?

Carl   Oh yeah.

Anthony   Nice.

Enter **Beth**.

Marc   Mum where you been?

Beth   Sorry love I.

My phone was out of battery.

I just . . .

What happened here /

Marc   How did you get my message then?

Beth   Got it just I went and charged it didn't I you know yeh.

Mason *goes for a cigarette.*

Hazel   Marc can you go and get some chocolate?

Get a quid from my purse yeh.

Marc   Yeh no.

OK.

He leaves.

A time. **Bernard** *is asleep.*

Anthony   Is he asleep?

Hazel   Yeh looks like it. He's not been too well.

He'll wake up for the choir practice though that's for sure.

Beth   Haz / el what's.

Hazel   Anthony can you give us a minute please?

Beth   You alright Hazel what happened?

They look at each other. Love.

Hazel   There was flooding . . .

So Gavin didn't speak to you.

Beth   What about.

Hazel   Yeh anyway you know that thing I said I'd do, I've really tried, I've not been able to do it?

Beth   Oh OK.

Hazel   Yeh they've said I'm not, suitable guardian, I can't look after Faith.

Beth   Thank you no thank you for trying (*she hugs her.*)

Hazel   There must be another way . . .

Long silence.

Beth   I might bring Faith's toys in.

Hazel   What.

Beth   They'll adopt her now.

I mean the social services.

Hazel   Don't say that.

Beth *sits down on the floor.*

Hazel   Obviously I mean she's upset the little one about what happened, in her past.

Beth *and* **Hazel** *look at each other, something breaks between them.* **Beth** *feels judged.*

Silence then no pauses:

Beth   Is Mason coming in?

Hazel   Yeh.

Beth   OK, great yeh.

Hazel   I mean.

Beth *gets up or moves.*

You can't lose hope yeh Beth like there are things we can do.

Beth   No no thank you Hazel.

They are stuck. **Hazel** *doesn't know what more to do. She's embarrassed somehow.*

Hazel   So we're gonna do the choir in a bit right?

Hazel *waves* **Anthony** *in from the entrance doors.*

Anthony   Can I come in yeh.

*Long silence. Community member (***Sunny***) walks in.*

Hazel   Hello I'm so sorry we aren't doing the lunch today but we have got some sandwiches.

Tharwa *and* **Tala** *enter,* **Tharwa** *speaks in Arabic,* **Tala** *replies in English. Community member (***Irene***) enters, and goes to make tea.*

Tharwa (*in Arabic*)   You're going to get sick look how wet you are!

Tala   I'm so wet! I'm shivering.

Hazel   Yeah she's really wet isn't she.

Tala   I'm so wet!

Tharwa (*in Arabic*)   Look at you come into the kitchen and dry off.

Hazel's *phone rings, she goes over to answer it.* **Anthony** *plays a few chords on the keyboard.*

Marc *enters.*

Tala   I want to go to the choir, Mum.

Tharwa (*in Arabic*)   First you need to get dry.

Tala   Please please please.

Tharwa (*in Arabic*)   Your hair is wet and you'll catch a cold.

Tala   I'm gonna sing! I don't care.

Tharwa (*in Arabic*)   It won't take me long though.

Tala   Please I really want to.

Tharwa (*in Arabic*)   It's not good to have wet hair in this weather.

Anthony   Hey.

Marc   Hey, how you doing?

Anthony   I'm good yeh.

Anthony   So . . . You gonna join today or /

Marc   I dunno man I haven't been here in ages.

Anthony   You should sing. I've been singing and you know Carl's been getting sick, yeh.

Marc   Sick, yeh.

Mason   Guys do me a favour, make some space for me.

Anthony   Yeh, Carl do me a favour and do this yeh. I'll take one more thank you very much.

Tala *runs across.*

Tharwa   Tala!

Tala   Can I have a solo?

Mason   Yes you can love.

Tala   Which part?

Mason   You know the bit we did it last week.

Tala   You promise.

Mason   Anthony get them lined up.

Anthony   Yeh. Carl, always in the right place /

Tala   I'm in front!

Anthony   Of course you are. Right here.

Tala   Mum!

Beth   Marc will join!

Marc *joins the line up.*

Anthony   Bernard, here.

Mason   Let's start with a hum, yeah? Give me that note there, you can go down there, or up there. Give me an 'Ahh'. You can do better.

Choir warms up, **Hazel** *enters.*

Mason   Y'alright Hazel?

Anthony   Hi Hazel.

Hazel   Yeah. You all look great.

Mason   OK /

Hazel   Um.

Sorry everyone. I.

I . . .

Hazel   Sing go on.

It's all good.

*A community member (***Leigh***) enters.*

Leigh   Sorry I'm late, Mason.

Chorus of hellos.

Mason   You all know your words. You got your words yeh.

Anthony   Marc doesn't.

Mason *hands out lyrics.*

Mason   Everyone else knows them yeah?

Tharwa   I need one.

Mason   Right. Just learn it yeh.

Tharwa   Sorry.

Mason   So everyone knows who's doing a solo. Tala, Bernard, yeah?

OK alright remember at the top.

'Wake up kids' let's really say the words let's really wake up with it yeh?

When we go to sing it outside them offices yeh, we want to be heard, yeh. OK.

Anthony   WAKE UP MARC.

Mason   I put a backing track down, but I've put some strings over today, so I'm gonna play some strings, don't let it throw you.

They begin to sing.

Mason   5, 6, 7, 8!

All *sing the first two verses of 'You Get What You Give' by New Radicals, until the line 'God's flying in for your trial'.*

Tala *sings 'But when the night is falling' solo, and* **Bernard** *sings 'You feel your tree is breaking / Just then' solo.*

All *come back in at 'You've got the music in you' and sing the chorus.*

Beth *begins to dance wildly.*

Fly
Fly
Fly
Fly

All

What's real can't die
Don't giv /

Beth *throws up suddenly.*

The singing comes to a stop. People don't know what to do, they stutter to a halt, and then slowly, to be improvised, they leave the space.

Hazel   OK everyone just give us a minute yeh.

Tala   Mum! She puked on the floor.

Tharwa (*in Arabic*)   Don't say that Tala leave her.

Mason   I'll /

Beth   SORRY sorry.

Marc   Mum.

Marc *thinks his mum has been drinking.*

Beth   Marc just give me a minute.

Beth *is ashamed.*

I'm so sorry I'm so sorry. Forgive me.

Bernard *comes over to* **Beth** *with a piece of tissue and begins to clean her mouth.*

Bernard   Perfect see . . .

Perfect.

Hazel *is nearby.*

Beth   I'm so sorry Hazel I'm sorry I didn't mean to let you down.

Hazel   I'm sorry.

I don't know what to do.

What we gonna do?

Long silence.

Beth   I'm sorry.

I'm just doing what I can with what I am.

Beat.

I just feel terrible that they stopped singing where's Mason?

Marc   Mum come on let's go home.

Beth   I don't want to go home.

Mason! Mason!

Hazel   She needs to go home.

Marc   Yeah I know. (*Following offstage*)

Beth   I feel terrible that they stopped.

Mason   Are you OK yeh?

Beth   Fine I just ate something weird I dunno.

Come back in here.

Mason   Alright OK.

Maybe we should . . .

Enter **Tharawa** *and* **Tala** *(couple of lines in Arabic)*

Enter **Carl**.

Enter **Anthony**.

Anthony   Marc. . . .

Marc   We're going home.

People are coming in . . .

Enter **Beth** *as she passes.*

Hazel   Do you want to just come here for a bit Beth?

Beth   No no it's fine.

It's fine.

I like the music.

Beth   Can you continue sorry yeh.

She laughs.

Marc   Mum let's go home.

Beth   I don't want to go.

Marc   Let's go.

Beth   I don't want to go!

Sunny   Fuck this (*exits*).

Mason   Yeh no it's OK? Like don't / worry if.

Beth   Nah nah it's all good seriously Leigh please stay.

To **Marc**.

Marc it's fine.

Let's stay a bit yeh please.

Mason   You OK /

Beth   Yeh I don't.

Mason   OK yeh alright.

Gather round then everyone yeh it's all good everyone's feeling better right yeh it's all good.

Beth   Come on Marc.

Sing!!! Sing a solo won't you?

Mason   OK.

Marc   No.

Mason   Come on. Do you remember when you came when you came to the choir we used to sing that Bob Marley tune 'Three Little Birds' yeh? Let's just do that.

Beth   Sing Marc please yeh for your mum?

Mason   Yeh OK everyone.

They all assent.

Mason   Marc?

Woke up this mornin',

All   Smiled with the risin' sun, . . . (*They continue to sing until and up to the line 'this is my message to you-ou-ou'.*)

Marc   Woke up this mornin', (*Continues to sing until and up to the line 'Sitting on my doorstep'.*)

Carl   Singin' sweet songs.
Of melodies pure and true,

All   Sayin', this is my message to you-ou-ou.

Beth *walks out, people start to drift.*

Anthony   I'm gonna go sorry, yeah sorry (*looks at* **Marc**).

Hazel   I think that's enough for today.

Mason *stops playing.*

Hazel   I'll drive you home, Carl, OK love?

Carl   Yeh.

Pause.

OK.

Marc   I'm going.

Mason   I'll lock up shall I Hazel?

Hazel   Thank you.

People leave.

Carl *goes with* **Hazel**.

Time passes, there is a long sequence of **Mason** *shutting down the community centre. He might play a bit on the piano.*

He goes in and out of the rooms, as he does, **Beth** *comes in so that when he comes back in she's there or she wanders in like she was looking for* **Hazel** – *she couldn't go home.*

Mason   Wow you scared me there.

What?

Where were you?

Beth   I just.

Mason   We thought you'd gone home.

Marc's gone after you.

You alright yeh.

Beth   No I.

There's like a church window or something fuck in there.

Mason   Yeh yeh no it's yeh . . . I mean!

Long silence.

Mason   Hazel's all gone I'm just locking up and that and yeh.

Beth   Thanks for erm getting Marc to sing and.

Mason   Come on it's all good d'you know what I mean.

Beth   You're alright Mason.

Mason   No / no come on it's all good I mean.

Beth   Yeh no /

Mason   Agh.

No yeh /

I mean.

Right.

Silence. **Mason** *tries to leave.*

I'd better I mean I'd better I've got to lock up?

Beth   Sorry I just didn't want to go home.

Mason   Is it because your ex / is.

Beth   No fuck no I just.

I don't want to.

I don't like being at home at the moment.

Mason   Right.

Beth   Her room, her bedroom is empty. And.

Mason   Yeh.

I mean I'm here for you if you need anything, Beth . . .

Silence.

Beth   I could really fucking use a drink to be honest.

Mason   Yeh no me too /

Beth   I'm just so fucking ski/nt.

They laugh like children.

Mason   Tell me about it yeh.

Beth   Me too but yeh / anyway it'd be nice to.

A noise above interrupts them, a bird in the roof.

Mason   Oh that's that bird. Fuck it scared me.

Beth   I hate that.

Shit.

They look up, the noise starts again.

I fucking hate that noise.

Make it stop.

Mason   I can't can I.

He waves ineffectually at the air.

It can't see me can it.

She laughs.

I know this is weird but.

So I mean did you ever get a lifebook, in care?

Beth   How did you know I / was in care.

Mason *looks at her, he knows.*

Beth   No.

No I mean, I didn't.

Beth   Yeh.

Pause.

Mason   Do you want to see mine?

Beth   What'd you just carry it around?

Fuck no.

I'm joking! Yeh!

Mason   Fuck.

I like looking at it.

Beth   Right no yeh.

Mason   It says all about me all about Mason.

Mason's life story book like.

She looks.

Mason   That was me in a foster family when I was ten, and that's actually at the park up the road?

Beth   Oh yeh I know that place.

Look at you!

Mason   That's when I was ten they took me to Butlin's. We moved. Then Fife. Yeh . . .

Beth   Oh yeh /

Mason   Thats my eighth foster family. There's a gap there, we lived near Loch Ness.

Beth   I was just in a home . . . I mean a few homes but I never had like a family. I mean a foster family.

Mason   Right oh . . . *(he goes to put the book away.)*

Beth   No go on.

Mason   Thats the penguins at the zoo. That's when we went on a train to go to Scarborough with my next foster father who was a baker. Yeh that's in then I mean there's gaps and stuff but.

Including like oh hang on – all these times with my mum – it's a bit fucked up actually.

The reason I stayed in the home was because my mum kidnapped me, she ran off and took me away.

Beth   No fucking way. Amazing.

Mason   Yeh.

He's a bit proud, he wonders whether he can go on, he goes on.

She was mental my mum was.

There was even an article in the paper and everything.

He hands her the book and recites. He knows it by heart.

'"No one is going to take my boy away from me" said the mother of little Mason, twelve, who she took away from his foster family last Friday evening, "He's my son and I love him and nothing is stronger than that."' Yeh that's the article it's cool / isn't.

Beth   .

He takes back the book.

Short silence.

Mason   She like kidnapped me and.

It was amazing we were by the seaside for six weeks we had sandwiches and.

It was incredible.

Beth   Wow.

Mason   Yeh. And like she was criticised for it and that but I know it's like.

What was really happening was that what was happening was that my mum was just proving that she loved me?

D'you know what I mean because my mum did love me.

D'you know what I mean deep down she did d'you know what I mean?

Long pause.

Beth *walks away.*

We went off and we had sandwiches and . . .

Beth   My mum . . .

Mason *doesn't react.*

Mason   I . . .

Pause.

Beth   Yeh she overdosed?

Mason   I'm so sorry.

Pause he looks away.

Beth   I found her.

Mason   How old were you?

Beth   You should come to contact with me.

Meet my daughter she'd love you.

She kisses him and grabs him. The way she knows how to show affection. He responds then moves away.

Beth   Do you want me to show you my tits?

She lifts her shirt.

Beth   Come on.

Mason   Nah I'm not /

Beth   Fucksakes / what is your problem?

Mason   Sure that's what you actually want like / you're upset and that.

Beth   I'm not upset.

Mason   Are you sure?

Makes a move towards her then backs away. Hesitates. Awkward.

Are you sure you're not just / because you're upset?

Beth   Mason Jesus live a little FUCKING CHRIST! / who cares.

Mason   AGHH!

Are you sure you want to because I'm not sure I don't want to if you're
not sure . . . I.

He kisses her.

She looks at him she begins to sing to him a song maybe one we've heard before.

Mason   What . . . you! You!!

*He sings with her – they are in love for a moment. They sing together . . . hold hands.
Look at each other. The streetlight shines through.*

They step away for a moment.

Beth   We could do . . .

We could do what your mum did and take her and go away Mason.

Mason Mason Mason.

Mason.

We could go away with her.

Mason   .

Beth   We could take her and / walk out of the contact.

Mason   Yeh.

Beth   Yeh?

Mason   Yeh.

Beth   I . . .

Mason   We could.

We can.

They kiss and hug but slowly, surely, **Beth** *moves away.*

We can do this.

Beth   What am I doing?

I can't.

I'm sorry.

Mason   OK.

We've gotta plan like.

Mason *tries to sing her into life he sings something.*

You can have all of me Beth . . .

Beth   I'm sorry Mason it's not /

Mason Take my body I'm all yours you can have every part of me you can have my arms my head my hand my cock my heart my leg you can destroy me have me or whatever you want you can / do to me.

Beat, he realises.

Beth I love you I fucking love you.

Beth *holds her chest.*

Beth I'm sorry I fucking don't know what I was doing . . . I just . . . I'm sorry. I need to go.

Mason No no fuck that stay with me . . . don't go don't go.

FUCK THEM. Beth, fuck them. FUCK FUCK FUCK FUCK!!!!!

Beth Yeh . . . Yeh yeh . . .

OK. OK.

They kiss again.

She pulls away.

Mason What the.

Beth I've got to go.

I'm sorry.

Beth *leaves.*

Silence. Enter **Bernard**. **Mason** *is startled.*

Mason Shit!

Bernard I'm just there in the corner don't mind me.

Mason Bernard.

Bernard Don't mind me.

Mason Mate what you doing?

Suddenly afraid.

Bernard Hazel said I could.

Just for a few.

Mason Mate. No. It's OK.

Bernard Sorry.

Sorry.

I get scared sometimes.

I get scared and I –. . . .

Mason   Yeh.

Yeh.

Blackout.

A lot of water falls in the dark.

Act Four: The first buds of spring

Four weeks later. The first days of spring. Garden flowers. The place has been sold. They are being tasked with moving out of it. Cardboard removal boxes are everywhere in the space.

The stage is emptier and during the course of the fourth act it is emptied entirely.

The concert has just taken place, two days before. **Hazel** *and* **Mason** *are in the kitchen,* **Mason** *is carrying big plastic bags full of stuff out and then coming back in.* **Hazel** *is dismantling things.*

Bernard *is in the garden steadily bringing the plants in and going back out to the garden.*

Hazel   What about the knives?

Maybe we could sell them.

Mason   Yeh maybe they're pretty new.

Bernard *coming in.*

Bernard   I'll put these here. For now.

Mason   Thanks Bernard, yeh I'll take them away / and.

Bernard   You'll find somewhere to plant them because if you don't I'll take them to the roundabout at night and plant them there in the middle.

Mason   No yeh. Sorry /

Bernard   People won't get at them there because the cars are going around and around you see.

Hazel   I'll put them out front of my house, maybe someone with a bit of space can take them.

Bernard *thinks about this.*

Bernard   OK.

He goes back to the garden.

Mason   I'm gonna need a hand with this.

(*laughs*) OK.

Hazel   This one's not ours.

That prayer group uses it I think they're just leaving it.

Mason   OK.

Bernard *brings more plants in.*

Beat.

Mason   Why don't I take what I've got over to your house?

Hazel   Leave it around the back.

Mason   OK I'll not be long yeh.

Hazel   Yeh.

Thanks Mason.

By the way I didn't tell you how much that concert was amazing.

It was amazing.

Well done yeh.

Mason   Oh thanks Hazel.

That really warms my heart.

Exit **Mason**.

Long silence.

Anthony *comes in,* **Bernard** *is awkward goes back to the garden.*

Hazel   Anthony.

What you doing here?

Anthony   Oh nothing yeh.

I was just coming to see if you needed any help.

Hazel   Oh! That's OK, we're nearly done.

It's all good love.

Hazel *goes on clearing things. A long silence, why is he still there?*

Drifts around. He's hungry.

Hazel   Do you want to eat something Anthony?

Anthony   Sure I mean, yeh.

Hazel   Let me see.

You're lucky we've not got round to clearing the fridge yet but that was next I was gonna take it all home and . . .

Yeh, OK.

She puts the soup to defrost in the microwave that still hasn't been taken out yet.

Sit down.

Anthony   Where sorry?

Hazel   Yeh.

They laugh.

Anthony   It's cool.

Thank you Hazel.

Hazel   Growing lad eh /

Anthony   Yeh.

He's wolfed it down Enter **Beth** *and* **Marc**. **Anthony** *is a bit ashamed and hides his food.*

Beth / Marc   Hi Anthony you alright?

Anthony   Yeh yeh.

I was just heading out.

See you Hazel. Thank you like /

Hazel   Anthony. . . /

Anthony   From the bottom of my heart.

He leaves.

Hazel   Hi Beth.

I didn't expect to see you here . . . I tried to call you . . . hi Marc.

Marc   Hi.

Beth   I just yeh I wanted to come here.

Hazel   Yeh . . . Yeh.

Silence they look around at how empty the place is.

Hazel   Yeh . . .

Beat.

Hazel   Marc that concert was amazing you were so great the solo and that.

Marc   Thanks . . . yeh . . . thanks Hazel.

Silence.

Beth   The music was so beautiful.

That bit when he sang 'Two Little Birds' / wow it was amazing it was amazing Hazel . . .

Marc   / Three little birds.

Hazel   Yeh though.

It moved mountains.

Marc   It's still closing though.

Hazel   Yeh I'm dropping the keys off this afternoon you came just in time.

Marc   Can I help?

Hazel   Yeh, OK yeh Mason will be back, put it out front yeh and he can load it up he'll be happy to see you.

Marc   OK.

He goes and begins to load the boxes away.

Hazel   I'm hopeful that there'll be another place.

Maybe.

Anyway I'm thinking of keeping the lunches going from my front room. If I'm allowed.

Beth   Yeh.

Silence.

Hazel   I mean I hope so . . .

You gotta hope right you know what I mean.

Yeh. Anyway.

Beth   Can I take this? It's such a beautiful flower.

Hazel   Oh yeh Bernard'll be happy you're taking that.

Beat. **Hazel** *wants to say so much.* **Marc** *comes back in during the following and overhears.*

Hazel   Beth?

Have you hear/d.

Beth   No but . . . we're going to court tomorrow.

Marc   And we're gonna get organised.

Beth   Yeh.

Marc   Over time and . . .

Beth   Yeh.

Marc   You know?

Marc   We're gonna fight . . .

Do you want me to take that?

Silence.

Beth   I love her so much. I will show her that fucking flower.

They're about to leave.

I wanted to come here because you make me feel better Hazel.

Hazel   Beth.

I . . .

As she's about to say something.

I'm just gonna go to the toilet.

Bernard *comes in and sees she's got the flower.*

Beth   I'm taking this is that OK?

Bernard   Yes.

He goes back out with the remaining plants to load them in the car.

Enter **Mason** *after a time. Huge awkwardness.* **Mason** *picks up some last bits and bobs.*

Beth   The singing was amazing Mason.

Mason   Cheers.

Yeh I thought we.

We were good.

It was good yeh.

Silence.

Mason   Yeh. I mean it's all growth /

Beth   Yeh . . .

Yeh no yeh it is isn't it (*laughs*).

Mason   Yeh, I mean . . . Fuck.

They look at each other and there is a long silence in which anything can happen. There is a small, barely perceptible swell in the sound and a physical impulse towards each other.

She shows her breasts again, as in Act 3 Scene 2. It's a kind of acknowledgement of something between them.

Then flush of the loo.

Mason   That's the last of it actually so I'm gonna go.

I'll call Hazel later, yeh. Sorry.

Looks around, like he did when he came in first time.

Bye then.

Beth   Goodbye . . .

Bernard *has come back in.* **Mason** *goes out.* **Hazel** *comes back in.*

Bernard   I put the plants in your backseat. Be careful with them.

Mason   OK mate. That's me done yeh. Thanks for your help.
Bye.

Bernard   Yes . . .

Beat. **Hazel** *comes out of the toilet – she goes to the pictures on the wall.*

Hazel   I'll come with you.

Tomorrow.

Beth   Thank you Hazel . .

Hazel *heads to the paintings.*

Bernard   You haven't taken the paintings down yet?

Hazel   My son did that one actually.

Bernard   Nice seascape.

Hazel   Yeh he'd not been to the sea when he drew that.

Beth *is about to leave.*

Beth.

I'm sorry that I didn't tell you the reasons I can't.

Be a guardian it's my son you see I'm sorry.

I put him in prison.

I'd just had enough you see he was taking my stuff and.

My son he attacked me.

I had enough of it you see.

So I thought if . . .

But I didn't know what he was actually into and.

So he got a long time . . .

They said I couldn't have Faith and Marcus in the house.

Beth   It's alright Hazel I.

Hazel   I wanted to help you I did.

I don't really know what to do.

I want to yeh . . .

Looks up.

He wanted a second chance.

I just.

What are we gonna do?

Beth   It's alright Hazel. I love you.

.

Hazel   Thank you.

I'm sorry (*I got emotional*).

Yeh.

Beth   Yeh I'll show her that flower. Hazel, look at it, it's so beautiful, it's like it's oh I just love it, wouldn't it be nice if you just had plants and trees around you when you woke up and that you just yeh, you just breathed them in like that.

I'm gonna. Marc . . . (**Beth** *exits*).

In silence: The room is totally empty by now – there is nothing left. By now it's an empty stage. **Hazel** *goes to put her coat on, and picks up the last bag,* **Bernard** *is sat on the last chair remaining like he doesn't want to go. He's looking round at the audience.* **Hazel** *goes to the kitchen, gets her bag and coat.*

Hazel   Bernard we better . . .

During the following the fourth wall is broken, **Bernard** *looks at the audience directly.*

Bernard   You know a long time ago . . .

I was in a relationship.

I mean I lived with a woman once. A long time ago she's not here now bless her.

We had fun.

Hazel   Yeh.

Bernard   Yeh it was . . . she was a funny person.

Made a lot of jokes.

Silence.

She'd use the sheet like you know on the bed, put it over her, pretended to be all sorts of animals she was very good she could make a rhino . . . (*he might do this, imitate a rhino, somehow*) or a fox yeh she'd just move into the sheet you know it wouldn't be a fox exactly but it there'd be something that she'd do that'd remind you of a fox? Then she'd use shadow, on the wall the shadows, you know like you felt like it WAS her dancing with a fox . . . she was so talented, she had so much . . . (*trails off*).

The lights are changing now to become more dramatic, theatrical, like a shadow play.

Anyway I think of her whenever I see a shadow . . . somehow. . .

Hazel   Thank you, Bernard.

Bernard   The concert was good.

You still didn't sing though.

Hazel   Me? No.

I haven't sung for decades.

Laughs.

You got good at it though or maybe you just were pretending.

Bernard   It's easy you just hesitate and then you do it for longer.

He does.

See.

Hazel *is looking down, at the floor.*

Hazel   No . . .

No I can't do that . . . nah Bernard.

Bernard (*to audience*)   Can you.

Help.

They all hum.

The whole theatre hums different people join in, there's a held note in the silence.

Hazel *still doesn't hum.*

Bernard *collects all but one of the remaining plants and heads out. As he does.*

I'm going then?

Hazel   .

Bernard   OK.

Thank you, sorry, bye.

He exits.

Hazel   Bye Bernard.

Hazel *is alone in the space, the lights are fading the drip is going. She looks at the audience. Slowly, she begins to sing. First a broken hum, then a hum, then an open note.*

Blackout.

End of play.

Acknowledgements for *Faith, Hope and Charity*

Thanks to: Alicia Fowles, Amber, Andre Verissimo, Andrew Lawton, Aso, ATD Fourth World, Ayodele Alaka, Bill Rashleigh, Bonny Downs Community Centre, Brixton Foodbank, Charly, Choir with No Name, Crisis, Dan Radley-Bennett, Dominic Cooke, Emily Lim, Eva Sajovic, Faye Merralls, Felicia, Fiona Banton, Flo Paul, Francesca Brady, Frank, Gleadless Valley Foodbank and Sheffield Foodbank Choir, Graham Sears, Icolyn Smith MBE, Janet Etuk, Sir James Munby, Jason Barnett, Jock, Kestral Theatre Company, Laura Richardson, Leah, Lindsey Crudden, Louise Tickle, Luke Clarke, Margaret Zeldin, Margeret O'Reilly, Marie Helene Estienne, Mary Campbell, Michael Morris, Molly, Molly Taylor, Natalie Burt, Natalie Dare, Nathaniel, National Theatre New Work Department, Niall McKeever and Grace Venning (*bursary design assistants*), Nickie, Oxford Community Soup Kitchen, Paul, Paula Lonergan, Peter Brook, Robert Wilkinson, Rose Montgomery, Michael Bryher, Sam Chaplin, Siblings Together, Sophie Humphreys OBE Pause Founder, The Spearhead Trust, Sybille, Tala Swareldahab, Tanya, Tawa, Waltham Forest Disability Resource Centre, Promela, Barbara, Linda, Wasim and Alan at the Waterloo Action Centre, Wellbeing Community Choir, Yonatan Pélé Roodner, Yo Tozer Loft, and the Young Vic Theatre. Special thanks to Annie – Surviving Safeguarding, and in memory of Jonny.

Reddish Brown

After 'The Rose That Grew From Concrete', by Tupac Shakur
Louis Armstrong's 'What A Wonderful World' by Bob Thiele and George Weiss
And Alexander Zeldin's *Faith, Hope and Charity*

As soon as I return to my rose coloured spectacles
my brown eyes become Hazel
I find Beth   she has Faith
whenever she remembers to.
You don't need to care about my friends;   I do.

Bernard will live out loud as surely as the sky is blue
because he is broken;
he is head-in-cloud   bearer
of inherited subclass haze
when his onion skin mould of carbon copy   shattered
he refused to be buried beneath the shards.
Instead, he climbs upon them   to dance-
brandishes his feet
                          with tapestries of survival
          he sees the world through hazel tinted shades.

          He sees trees raised through concrete
          (Alongside) roses born blue
          He blossoms carelessly before us
          This world can be wonderful, it's true-

                              The leaking roof   is waterfall
          Let Tala swim.
                              Anthony met his Mark
                    It's beautiful
                                                            Let love win.
                    I see Mason-ettes at the other end of ladders
                    I am not set up to climb;
Let pipe dreams   be my mountains
Let satellites   be my stars
Deprive   me   of   your   promises
          Render fairy tales   no less
                    Than our resource   of a looking glass.
                    We   will   be   okay
I sink into the carols of my community
draw reality out of their tune
help hazel raise the tint of my spectacles
let the world be rosy
whenever I remember to.

The Seeing Place

The Inequalities writer and director, Alexander Zeldin, in an interview with Faye Merralls, producer of A Zeldin Company, and editor of this volume, conducted in July 2021.

FM Where do you start? Or perhaps this is more accurately asked as: where do you finish? When a production has opened and then closed, what is next? How do you land on what to work on? And thus, where do you then start?

AZ It's a difficult question because it's hard to always pin-point where to start. When I think of the beginnings of a new idea or a new process, I am reminded of the Japanese phrase 'Jo-ha-Kyū', which Peter Brook and Marie-Hélène Estienne have drummed into me as a sort of mantra for many years. It can be translated, or interpreted, as 'beginning', 'development' and 'culmination'. And in every jo-ha-kyū there is another beginning-development-culmination, like a Russian doll. It applies to the way an actor moves onstage: a thought or a movement starts, it develops, culminates and inside the culmination – the kyū – is the seed for the next beginning.

Being attentive to the new beginning can be very difficult because we listen to outside forces, or an opportunity might present itself from within the industry. These are okay ways to find the new beginning, but it makes it harder to listen to what's really truthful. I tend to try and stick to one principle, which is led by what I feel is most raw inside me and what would be most risky. For example, when I started *Faith, Hope and Charity*, I felt so deeply about a mother whose child had been taken – there was a video replaying in my head that I had seen of a child being snatched from its parents. That really resonated within me, something felt very raw so I knew that would be a good starting place for the play.

Alongside that, as I am gaining more experience, I am also trying to think about how I can move the form of theatre I'm trying to do forward; to develop my practice as a whole. Rather than just thinking about an idea for a singular play or narrative, I like to ask myself: how can I push the form I am working in forward? Often that comes from going back to the history and origins of the theatre and learning about how and why theatre has been made in the past, whilst simultaneously looking at it afresh with eyes that have the knowledge of the production that I have just done.

FM What do you mean by the 'form' of theatre you are working in?

AZ I am interested in being in a dialogue with what's come before. I am interested in understanding the ways in which people have needed theatrical expression. I think you can live your life asking the question – 'what is theatre?' – and that question has to be constantly asked and never completely answered. 'What is theatre?' is a not unlike 'what is faith?'; 'what is love?'; 'what is life?'. It's an ambitious question you have to keep asking. And at the same time, you have to be asking yourself: how can I express how I feel about the world? So you have to be simultaneously in the present in a very simple, immediate, non-intellectual way but also I like to try and deepen my feeling of what theatre is through looking to the past.

I was looking at medieval staging the other day with Natasha [Jenkins, Set and Costume Designer], and we were looking at the different platforms they would use and how people moved around them. And I think it's exciting to see how theatre was done then and you can look into what they were trying to achieve with their form, and how that might teach you something about what you are trying to achieve now. The lessons of the past are useful not to think directly about where we are now but to think about how we can move forward.

FM   You mentioned a video that you saw about a child that was being taken away from their mother, as a starting point for *Faith, Hope and Charity*. Can you talk more about your research process that underpins your writing?

AZ   Research material can be from anywhere: sometimes it's from the lives of others; sometimes it's from literature; sometimes it's from my own life. I often find that a documentary source – so long as it's not a documentary that isn't already loaded with artistic meaning or intention – is very powerful.

I mostly steer clear of contemporary plays as references, or modern theatrical material but, as I'm writing, I often read what are considered to be the more classic plays.

And then alongside that, as a paradox, I like to look at very contemporary images, reports, youtube videos, moments I observe on the street and to conduct interviews with people through charitable organisations. I like to look at contemporary life through a kind of classical lens. That's why I like to start with the very raw, emotional material that is not yet shaped into anything specific.

FM   What does the experience of reading mean to you, and to your theatre?

AZ: I was listening to an interview with Lars von Trier in which he said that for him the first art is/was literature. And I agree with that; it is for me too.

I can trace my inner building of myself as a person through some of the books I have read.

Literature is the art form that most informs me, and it opens up new territories in understanding what it is to be a human being. Having the resonance of great literature – whether you're making theatre, cinema, a painting, a song – is helpful.

I also think some of the most original art, right now, at least as far as I can tell, some of the most form-pushing art, is in literature, through writers such as: Karl Ove Knausgaard, Annie Ernaux, John Keene, Rachel Cusk, Maggie Nelson.

FM   Do you see any similarity in the experience of a reader reading a book, and an audience member watching one of your plays, or a play in general?

AZ   I think when you read a book there is a very deep solitude, a private moment with the world of the book, which then travels and echoes in you, in a multi-faceted way, and etches its way into life, into the feeling, the rhythm of the way we experience reality, and thus, life with others. And when you look at a great painting, it is showing its world to you privately and then to you as part of a community along with the other gallery attendees, but at the moment of watching, of seeing, the painting is for you privately. Painting is the other art form that is very important to me.

A great work of literature or a great painting invites you to consider your roles as an individual in a wider context. I want an experience in the theatre that is complex, and that is multi-faceted, and that is incredibly intimate.

FM   This is quite a big question: you start with your research – the books you are reading alongside the people you are meeting – how do you get from there to opening night? What do you do in rehearsals?

AZ   It's changed over the years. For the play I'm doing now, for instance, I'm doing some research workshops in care homes with actors present, but then I'm sending a full, finished script ahead of rehearsals with no workshops in between. For this trilogy there was much more to and fro between the workshops and the writing process. As a general rule, I need to write a lot on my own to begin with. And often the beginning is prose, and description before I move into dialogue. And then I take what I have written into a room with actors: we work with that text, we improvise on top of that text and then I go back and write again. I like to know who the actors are, to begin to shape the character in a conversation with them, in observing them, listening to them.

Then, the biggest thing is that I try not to be finished, I try not to shut any avenue down, I leave things as open as possible. In other words: I think a question is more living than an answer. When something is answered, it feels dead. That applies to every aspect: the writing, the directing, the designing, I am trying to make it feel like it is still being born for as long as possible. I want a play to feel like it is still being born beyond opening night.

The majority of the words are of course fixed earlier on, and more and more what I write in the first few months is what ends up being onstage more or less, but I want people to feel like it's going to keep on changing, because it creates a sense of a search and in that search unexpected things happen.

As for a theatre process, I think theatre is a way of bringing people closer to life. It can help us to break the barriers of fear, confusion and so on that we put up between us and the world, between us and people who we see as different, between our sense of ourselves and the mystery inside us. When I am working with an actor, my question is always: what barriers is that person putting up? How can this person take something away? How can we get to the core, the core of what we can do together in the theatre?

The process in the rehearsal room is also linked to something very personal. For example, when I think about *LOVE*, and the situation in *LOVE*: while I was in rehearsals I was always thinking of my mother getting older, but also my father, my father being ill and me watching him as he deteriorated physically so rapidly. I experienced a very complex feeling of love in response to that which I very much couldn't express at that time in my life – and I wanted the character of Colin to express that. So until I had that feeling in the *LOVE* rehearsals – of watching that and being able to feel that same or similar feeling as watching my father – I just kept on going. Whenever I feel that anything onstage is in any way lying, I go to war on it until it feels alive, until the feeling I get from watching it onstage is the same as the feeling I have inside myself, the feeling of being alive.

FM You've mentioned a little here about how you work with the actors, but how do you find the actors in the first place? What do you look for?

AZ It is very valuable for me to have a mixture of people in my casts; people who have acted, and have lots of experience, and people who haven't so much but who have a kind of expertise to bring from life. That's because I am looking for an actor to not rely on anything they have done previously. I need anyone that works with me to be needing to take a big risk artistically and go into the unknown, whatever that unknown is for them. But I find that most of the great theatre actors that I have had the privilege to work with on this trilogy often seek out work that pushes them into something they haven't done. They are looking to risk something.

When I first met Hind Swareldahab, who has become somebody very important to me and my work, we did a tightrope exercise: imagining you're walking on a tight rope and meeting somebody on the end of the tight rope who you haven't seen in many years. Hind had, and has, a lot of feelings about people she hasn't seen in many years because of her situation, having been far from Sudan for so long, and the way she articulated that was through her body, through how she walked that tightrope. The exercise helped her say something she couldn't say otherwise, therefore the theatre helped her say that something, she needed the theatre to express that. She walked that tightrope with such conviction that I was really moved by it, and I thought: this is somebody who needs the theatre and understands that the theatre can touch them very deeply, in a very honest way. She had never acted or really even been in a theatre before and had absolutely no preconception of what theatre is, or should be. She has since become an actor, so I no longer talk of her as a 'non professional'.

FM The plays within this volume have all have been made with the same creative team. Can you tell me a bit more about that process? Is that significant to the outcome of the shows? How do you all work together?

AZ Natasha [Jenkins] was originally a stage manager and also assistant director and then a director in her own right, so she had many strings to her bow. She really began becoming a designer full-time from when we started work on *Beyond Caring*; she had done a few things beforehand but that process of growing creatively into her role as a designer began for us together on this work, and it was very powerful as we were so deeply in sync. She has now gone on to design many, brilliant things with other directors and will continue doing that, but what we created together was an approach to space that was also a result of her own particular sensitivity and talent and the fact that she hadn't got ingrained ways of doing things. What I loved about Nat was that in our work she often only spoke about life, never about theatre or design. And as a result, her designs are insanely rigorous. It raises the bar for me, as she won't accept anything being a lie. Anything just representing something, each thing on stage has to have a life of its own. Also, when we started, our roles were very fluid; she was doing so many things to hold the chaos together and give it shape, that our collaboration was born out of that, not out of a well-worn practice or ingrained habits about how things should be done.

It's a similar situation with Josh Anio Grigg. Josh was a DJ and Artist and a show we did at East 15 called *Butterfly Soup* was one of his first jobs doing sound for theatre. Again, I wanted to work with somebody who wasn't weighed down by the contemporary expectations in the theatre but who was an artist I loved the energy of. And Josh's own approach is more that of someone who makes performances, who is collaborating on the performance as a whole, but who has a particular skill to bring in sound. Indeed, alongside his work as a sound designer, he creates installations and environments for parties and happenings. When we first worked together on *Butterfly Soup* (based on *Elephant* by Gus Van Sant) I didn't want a sound designer but a live DJ for the show. And when we started thinking of *Beyond Caring*, we originally thought Josh would be there live, doing the sound effects alongside the show. Nowadays, I just send him a message with a few words about the show and then he creates sounds, and then he shows up to rehearsals and something great happens.

And Marc Williams wasn't working as a lighting designer at the time, but rather in-house at the National Theatre, so he could choose what he did freelance and only do a certain number of shows he cared deeply about a year. I deliberately started working with people that weren't already heavily established in their field, I wanted people that would build something with me.

And the way we all work together is: I have them present from the beginning of the workshops, or on visits around the country. For instance, we all went to Sheffield to the food banks together for *Faith, Hope and Charity*. Josh would record ambient sound, Marc would think about how the space is lit, and Nat would photograph every light-switch and skirting board. We go on a shared adventure as I'm writing and developing the play. Then during rehearsals, we don't discuss things all that much, as there is a shared understanding of what we set out to make and each person does their part but also feeds in and contributes to the other areas in a collective spirit.

I was once given a piece of advice from a French director and writer whom I very much admire: try to work with people that are good for you, that care about you, and that you care about. And that's definitely how I tried to set up this team.

FM   Continuing on the theme of collaborators, can you tell me more about the other people that work on these projects with you? I am referring to the people who become the centre of your research, who help you grow the situations that appear onstage.

AZ   Theatre is a catalyst for different people to meet, people who wouldn't ordinarily meet each other.

In *Faith, Hope and Charity* we involved nearly one hundred people with experiences similar to those of the characters in the play. I think it is important that people feel involved with a production that is in some way built on things that have been witnessed by and with them.

We worked with Oxford Community Soup Kitchen, Bonny Downs Community Centre, Waterloo Action Centre, a food bank in Sheffield and their choir. We as a team would volunteer in these places, sometimes doing some improvisations in their spaces, and then people from there might come into rehearsals and observe. We also collaborated with a family court and did a whole trial in character there.

In Chicago, I had the Chicago Workers Collaborative come in and direct the script of *Beyond Caring* for a day. In this way, there's a sense of something shared in terms of the creation of the piece. The model is one of porousness between the world and the theatre – and that needs to be aggressively fought for to retain that authentically collaborative process.

This way of doing things is at the root of what theatre is – it goes back to the history again. Theatre has always been a means for different members of society to come together and share more deeply than they would be able to do otherwise without the theatre. When theatre stops being that it needs to be forcefully re-started to do just that.

FM   Tell me more about the space, and the design process.

AZ   I think Bernard-Marie Koltès once said in an interview something along the lines of: 'There are some spaces in the world that are more than spaces they are metaphors of something about the world'.

The loading bay of a factory in the middle of the night where a few strangers come to meet each other and work together is a theatrical situation of our time. A situation involves a place. I think there are certain places in life that have a kind of unique energy. And I wanted to put those on stage at certain points. If we ever get the opportunity to play the whole trilogy side by side in one event, you would see these three spaces and how they echo each other and in a way it should give a portrait of society.

FM   Moving offstage, do you think about the audience at all during the process and if so, when and how?

AZ   I think about them all the time. In the very first rehearsals I have seats onstage and I ask people to sit in them so that when we are making a bit of action on stage, we are already thinking about the way it is going to be witnessed and watched. It's why I really struggle in small rehearsal rooms – they don't account for how the audience are going to witness it. For me the audience is an active, living part of the process the whole time and I don't really see a separation between a stage and the audience in a way that rehearsal rooms enforce.

Maybe it's very obvious but as soon as I start making a play, I am thinking about where the audience are going to sit, how they are going to watch. The origin of the word theatre after all means 'seeing place' so: where are you going to see it from?

FM   Before a performance, I have often heard you say to the actors: 'let the audience witness you', and 'witness' is a word that gets repeated through your process. What do you mean by that? Are the connotations to a court of law, and indeed to justice, in any way significant?

AZ   There's something very powerful about 'being seen'. If you are witnessed, it means that you are being seen and if someone is being seen then it means someone is making an effort to watch you. I like using words that are active, and witness is an active word.

I like using it with actors because to say they are being witnessed it can make one feel cared about and 'seen' and acknowledged so they don't need to overact, or oversell their character. I want something to be a bit more contained, not over-acted.

I don't have the final word on anything to do with our work. We make it and people can think whatever they want about it. I want to make something in order for it to have its own resonance. I don't want to control how it is interpreted or understood.

FM   What do you want the audience to witness?

AZ   I guess I want the really invisible things to become seen. Harold Pinter spoke powerfully about the idea that theatre takes us *behind* the mirror of our time. So theatre doesn't reflect back what we see, it shows us something that is behind what we see. I really feel closely connected to that.

FM   And another word that you use regularly, and has come up in other interviews you have done, is 'dignity'. Why? What do you mean by 'dignity'? And why is it relevant and important to theatre?

AZ   The most important thing for a person is to feel understood, humans need to feel seen and understood. There is a very powerful thing in almost every religious tradition when an angel appears or when a god appears – and what's really happening here is someone being seen. In the history of art the gaze is, of course, very powerful, the very idea of looking. In theatre, it is important to acknowledge that a person is seen. In these productions, we keep the lights on all the time, the actors are in the same lighting state as the audience, and thus we are all given an opportunity to be seen.

And, in turn, when you see someone else you must acknowledge that you are seeing them, without all the fanfare of convention or representation or sentimentality. I'm after the moment when you see someone, and acknowledge them: that becomes a moment of dignity. Truly watching someone and seeing someone, not turning away, is about dignity.

FM   What for you are the conditions to make theatre in?

AZ   Famously Peter Brook once said that if you get a person to walk across an empty space with another person watching then that's theatre.[1] I think that has been in my heart since I was fifteen. That's the miracle of theatre. Theatre doesn't need a house, theatre doesn't need a home or an institution, although those things are good and have a place. But really, theatre isn't a building or a stage and certainly not an industry, theatre is about a way of looking at the world that has existed for thousands of years and is constantly being renewed. The conditions are inside us all the time and they just need another person. Those are the two conditions of theatre: what's inside us and the need for another person or another group of people.

FM   What happens after opening night?

AZ   Opening night is always a moment of release for people, but I usually do keep working on it. I don't like to stop there. And then touring and reviving enables even more work on the production.

What I love about touring internationally is that you're opening in a different city every week and you have to change the play for each city, and for each space, otherwise it doesn't work. Opening night is just part of a journey. It is not always seen that way in the British and American tradition. In America, I was not allowed to give notes directly to the actors after opening night, they went through the Stage Manager. It is like what I said about rehearsals, something needs to be constantly living, you always need to be going somewhere. The illusion of an opening night is that it is fixed and finished – not at all, it needs to keep growing. It is a nice moment to celebrate a step on the journey, but there is still much work to do. This work can, however, sometimes be done without me! So it's usually a good idea to go away for a couple of days after opening night and that's a habit I am trying to get into.

FM   The plays in this volume have all toured, have all been performed in more than one venue in the UK and abroad, and you and I have set up a theatre company specifically to try to build tours for your work. Why is that such an important part of the process for you?

AZ   Bob Dylan is a really interesting artist to refer to in giving an answer to that question. Why does he keep touring? I assume he doesn't need the money, he doesn't need the acclaim and yet he was still touring extensively (pre-Covid) at the age of eighty. I think it is just what you have to do, it's part of a tradition: theatre has to tour, you're a travelling player. The very DNA of the theatre is that it should travel, you bring the show to a different audience, a different community, a different city, a different language. Streaming to other cities isn't the same. Internationalism is a very important part of touring – we now live in a global world that is extremely interconnected despite Brexit's best attempts to make us feel like it isn't, and there's a way of affirming what kind of connection we want with others by touring theatre. It's a way of saying: we want to meet you, let's get to see something about each other.

FM   Why theatre? Why do you present your characters and situations in the medium of theatre?

AZ   I have to, I am in love with theatre, it's a faith, it's a way to live. I also hope it's a way to be useful. Many great artists before have shown us that the art of theatre can be refreshed and rejuvenated for now, for the time that we are in. I want to try and do that. A perhaps immodest, but entirely sincere ambition. I want to deeply commit to an ancient art form. I need to do that selflessly though: you need to give yourself to theatre, it can't be all about you, it won't work.

FM   And finally, what do you think is the future of theatre? And your theatre?

AZ   I am very optimistic about the future of theatre. Theatre exists in a kind of tension. Theatre progresses through a friction of people saying 'everything is shit, I am going to show you how I am going to do it' and those same people can then get considered shit and be shown how to do it. In that friction, that is often accompanied by both rage and love, there is a renewal.

Note

1   From the opening of *The Empty Space,* by Peter Brook: 'A man walks across this empty space whilst someone is watching him, and this is all that is needed for an act of theatre to be engaged.'

Epilogue
Peter Brook and Marie-Hélène Estienne

When we met Alexander Zeldin he was, maybe, twenty-one years old. David Lan, who ran the Young Vic at the time, had followed his work and recommended him to us.

We met a young man full of ideas and passion and will – but he was flying off to Naples to work on *Romeo and Juliet* and we only saw him again a couple of years later.

At that point, it became obvious that he must work with us. And so he did, becoming a wonderful assistant director on our work on 'a magic flute', which toured the world. Then he was gone again.

The next we heard, he invited us to a play. It was *Beyond Caring*, and it was a revelation. This young man had theatre flowing through him and he showed a side of it that was carved as if from life itself. It was heart-breaking. Since then, we have been companions to each other on our respective searches. And the rest of the story is here, with *LOVE, Faith, Hope and Charity*, told by those who have supported and cherished this work of his, of which we are so proud.

2021

CPSIA information can be obtained
at www.ICGtesting.com
Printed in the USA
LVHW020229220423
745015LV00004B/227